THE CHRISTIAN MORAL COMPASS

Paul J. Headington

Kingdom Publishers

Copyright© Paul J Headington 2024

All rights reserved. No part of this book may be reproduced in any form by photocopying or any electronic or mechanical means, including information storage or retrieval systems, without permission in writing from both the copyright owner and the publisher of the book. The right of Paul J Headington to be identified as the author of this work has been asserted by him in accordance with the Copyright, Designs and Patents Act 1988 and any subsequent amendments thereto.

A catalogue record for this book is available from the British Library.

All scripture quotations have been taken from the New King James version of the Bible and where illustrated, by the Voices for Justice UK (online materials)

ISBN: 978-1-916801-12-7

1st Edition 2024 by Kingdom Publishers, London, UK.

You can purchase copies of this book from any leading bookstore or email contact@kingdompublishers.co.uk

I dedicate my book to my loving wife Hayley, my beautiful daughter, & in loving memory to my parents John and June.

Holy Bible (New King James Version)

2 Timothy 4:1-5

1 "I charge *you* therefore before God and the Lord Jesus Christ, who will judge the living and the dead at His appearing and His kingdom: ² Preach the word! Be ready in season *and* out of season. Convince, rebuke, exhort, with all longsuffering and teaching.

3 For the time will come when they will not endure sound doctrine, but according to their own desires, because they have itching ear, they will heap up for themselves teachers; ⁴ and they will turn *their* ears away from the truth, and be turned aside to fables. ⁵ But you be watchful in all things, endure afflictions, do the work of an evangelist, fulfil your ministry.

Table of Contents

Foreword		9
CHAPTER 1	Introduction	13
CHAPTER 2	GOD	17
CHAPTER 3	Christian Principles & Values	31
CHAPTER 4	Establishment of The Christian Church	41
CHAPTER 5	The Decline of Christian Values and Morals	51
	The Church of England	
	Political, Cultural & Social Pressures	
	Political – Health Service	
	Political – The Environment	
	The Monarchy	
	The Lord of the Storm	
CHAPTER 6	False Religions and Occults	153
CHAPTER 7	References	173

Foreword

This book has been written to enable the reader to understand the importance of the Christian faith, through those established principles, values and morals (given to us by God); that we must all adhere to every day; throughout our lives.

We are living in a time where Christian principles and values are in decline - through false preaching of the Christian faith (particularly by the Church of England and Christian denomination churches); the English Monarchy, the establishment of multi-faith groups, and the changes made by successive governments – all opposing the core Christian principal laws and values which were meant to protect the national population, but now seek to make long term damage to the fabric of society.

However, we must acknowledge that God is still in control, and loves all those who truly believe on Him through His Son Jesus Christ. God wants a relationship with each individual, as He created you and everyone born into this world, from the very beginning (Adam), to the very end until Jesus Christ returns.

Therefore, it is important that you (the reader), and everyone to accept Jesus Christ as Lord and Saviour in their lives, turning to Him with all your heart, asking for forgiveness for your sins, so that you can inherit eternal life.

This book will cover:

1. **Introduction:** God's love of this world - The History of Creation, The Garden of Eden, The Temptation and Fall of Man

2. **God**: Omnipotence, Omnipresence, Omniscience & Omnibenevolence

3. **The Christian Principles and Values**

4. **The Establishment of The Christian Church**

5. **The Decline of Christian Values and Morals**:

    - The Church of England
    - Political, Cultural and Social Pressures
    - Political: The National Health Service
    - Political: The Environment; and
    - The Monarchy

6. **False Religions and Occults**

I ask the reader to review and examine the pattern of events which have been described in this book, and the impact they are happening within the UK; and any similarities abroad (i.e. particularly the United States of America, North and South American countries, Asian nations, the European Union, Eastern European countries, Middle Eastern Countries, African nations, China, Japan, Australia, New Zealand, etc.)

You will be very surprised to see the escalation of unnatural, ungodly (wicked) practices occurring at a time when national and global unrest is growing. However, God has already prophesised the events which will come about, before Jesus Christ returns to judge the whole world. Are you ready? Do you believe in Him?

I hope you enjoy reading this book.

Please note all biblical verses and texts are from the New Kings James Version Bible (NKJV).

Also, I would like to thank **Voices for Justice UK (VFJUK, www.vfjuk.org)** for granting permission to use its online materials for this publication.

Glory to God!

CHAPTER 1

Introduction

God's love for His world is evidenced from the very beginning of creation. God created everything (for His own pleasure and plans) within six days.

This is illustrated in **Genesis Chapter 1 (NKJV)**, setting out the history of creation, and **Chapter 2 (NKJV)** covers the area where God created and placed Adam and Eve; in The Garden of Eden.

Christians acknowledge that sin was mankind's downfall, caused by the disobedience of Adam and Eve; not following God's instruction(s), and therefore, rebelling against Him by believing a lie from Satan, the serpent (**Genesis 3, NKJV**).

Therefore, I encourage you to read the book of **Genesis**, particularly **Chapters 1 to 3:** *The History of Creation, The Garden of Eden and The Temptation and Fall of Man.*

There has been a rapid decline of morality within the world, where once held Christian beliefs and values were respected within the United Kingdom and the World; the Monarchy, Governments (including departments), Political parties, denominations of Christian churches, Educational Sector, the National Health

Service and health care institutions, HM Court and Tribunal Service, Police Service and the Armed Forces, etc.

Since the fall of mankind and in every year which has passed, the whole world (citizens) has rebelled against God, in heart and action, accepting to sin through choice, taking us further away from Him, God (**1 John 3:8, NKJV** *"He who sins is of the devil, for the devil has sinned from the beginning. For this purpose, the Son of God was manifested, that He might destroy the works of the devil"*).

It is through God's Grace that we can be saved through faith; **Ephesians 2:8-10 (NKJV)** *[8]"For by grace you have been saved through faith, and that not of yourselves; it is the gift of God, [9] not of works, lest anyone should boast, [10] For we are His workmanship, created in Christ Jesus for good works, which God prepared beforehand that we should walk in them"*.

God's love for the entire world is clearly seen and illustrated, **John 3:15-21 (NKJV):**

[15] that whoever believes in Him should not perish but have eternal life. [16] For God so loved the world that He gave His only begotten Son, that whoever believes in Him should not perish but have everlasting life. [17] For God did not send His Son into the world to condemn the world, but that the world through Him might be saved.
[18] "He who believes in Him is not condemned; but he who does not believe is condemned already, because he has not believed in the name of the only begotten Son of God. [19] And this is the condemnation, that the light has come into the world, and men

loved darkness rather than light because their deeds were evil. [20] For everyone practicing evil hates the light and does not come to the light, lest his deeds should be exposed. [21] But he who does the truth comes to the light, that his deeds may be clearly seen, that they have been done in God."

CHAPTER 2

GOD

In my last book titled *"God's Promises Fulfilled: The End Times Prophecy"*, I covered, What is God like?

This chapter will now concentrate on four aspects of God, providing biblical verses and texts to help illustrate to the reader that:

- **God is Omnipotence**
- **God is Omnipresence**
- **God is Omniscience**
- **God is Omnibenevolence**

Numbers 23:19 (NKJV)
[19] *"God is not a man, that He should lie,*
Nor a son of man, that He should repent.
Has He said, and will He not do?
Or has He spoken, and will He not make it good?

1. GOD IS OMNIPOTENCE

The term omnipotence refers to the idea that God is all-powerful. There are many stories in the Bible that reveal the power of God.

An example of God's omnipotence is found in **Genesis 1, Job 38 and Revelation 19 (NKJV)** which describes His power and glory over all creation.

Job 38 (NKJV), The Lord Reveals His Omnipotence to Job

38: 1 *Then the Lord answered Job out of the whirlwind, and said:*
² *"Who is this who darkens counsel*
By words without knowledge?
³ *Now prepare yourself like a man;*
I will question you, and you shall answer Me.
⁴ *"Where were you when I laid the foundations of the earth?*
Tell Me, if you have understanding.
⁵ *Who determined its measurements?*
Surely you know!
Or who stretched the line upon it?
⁶ *To what were its foundations fastened?*
Or who laid its cornerstone,
⁷ *When the morning stars sang together,*
And all the sons of God shouted for joy?
⁸ *"Or who shut in the sea with doors,*
When it burst forth and issued from the womb;
⁹ *When I made the clouds its garment,*
And thick darkness its swaddling band;
¹⁰ *When I fixed My limit for it,*
And set bars and doors;
¹¹ *When I said,*
'This far you may come, but no farther,
And here your proud waves must stop!'
¹² *"Have you commanded the morning since your days began,*
And caused the dawn to know its place,

¹³ That it might take hold of the ends of the earth,
And the wicked be shaken out of it?
¹⁴ It takes on form like clay under a seal,
And stands out like a garment.
¹⁵ From the wicked their light is withheld,
And the upraised arm is broken.
¹⁶ "Have you entered the springs of the sea?
Or have you walked in search of the depths?
¹⁷ Have the gates of death been revealed to you?
Or have you seen the doors of the shadow of death?
¹⁸ Have you comprehended the breadth of the earth?
Tell Me, if you know all this.
¹⁹ "Where is the way to the dwelling of light?
And darkness, where is its place,
²⁰ That you may take it to its territory,
That you may know the paths to its home?
²¹ Do you know it, because you were born then,
Or because the number of your days is great?
²² "Have you entered the treasury of snow,
Or have you seen the treasury of hail,
²³ Which I have reserved for the time of trouble,
For the day of battle and war?
²⁴ By what way is light diffused,
Or the east wind scattered over the earth?
²⁵ "Who has divided a channel for the overflowing water,
Or a path for the thunderbolt,
²⁶ To cause it to rain on a land where there is no one,
A wilderness in which there is no man;
²⁷ To satisfy the desolate waste,
And cause to spring forth the growth of tender grass?
²⁸ Has the rain a father?

Or who has begotten the drops of dew?
²⁹ From whose womb comes the ice?
And the frost of heaven, who gives it birth?
³⁰ The waters harden like stone,
And the surface of the deep is frozen.
³¹ "Can you bind the cluster of the Pleiades
Or loose the belt of Orion?
³² Can you bring out Mazzaroth in its season?
Or can you guide the Great Bear with its cubs?
³³ Do you know the ordinances of the heavens?
Can you set their dominion over the earth?
³⁴ "Can you lift up your voice to the clouds,
That an abundance of water may cover you?
³⁵ Can you send out lightning's, that they may go,
And say to you, 'Here we are!'?
³⁶ Who has put wisdom in the mind?
Or who has given understanding to the heart?
³⁷ Who can number the clouds by wisdom?
Or who can pour out the bottles of heaven,
³⁸ When the dust hardens in clumps,
And the clods cling together?
³⁹ "Can you hunt the prey for the lion,
Or satisfy the appetite of the young lions,
⁴⁰ When they crouch in their dens,
Or lurk in their lairs to lie in wait?
⁴¹ Who provides food for the raven,
When its young ones cry to God,
And wander about for lack of food?

Revelation 19:6 NKJV

And I heard, as it were, the voice of a great multitude, as the sound of many waters and as the sound of mighty thunderings, saying, "Alleluia! For the Lord God Omnipotent reigns! Let us be glad and rejoice and give Him glory, for the marriage of the Lamb has come, and His wife has made herself ready."

2. <u>GOD IS OMNIPRESENCE</u>

God's omnipresence means that He is present everywhere, all the time. His presence is not limited by time or space. Because God created the universe, He is above all things and holds all things together, we see this in the following Old and New Testament biblical (NKJV) verses:

<u>OLD TESTAMENT verses</u>

Deuteronomy 31:6 - *Be strong and of good courage, do not fear nor be afraid of them; for the Lord your God, He is the One who goes with you. He will not leave you nor forsake you."*

Psalm 139:1-3
139 O Lord, You have searched me and known me.
² You know my sitting down and my rising up;
You understand my thought afar off.
³ You comprehend my path and my lying down,
And are acquainted with all my ways.

Proverbs 15:3 - *The eyes of the Lord are in every place, Keeping watch on the evil and the good.*

Job 34:21 - *"For His eyes are on the ways of man, And He sees all his steps.*

Isaiah 57:15 - *For thus says the High and Lofty One*
Who inhabits eternity, whose name is Holy:
"I dwell in the high and holy place,
With him who has a contrite and humble spirit,
To revive the spirit of the humble,
And to revive the heart of the contrite ones.

Jeremiah 23:24 - *Can anyone hide himself in secret places, So I shall not see him?" says the Lord; "Do I not fill heaven and earth?" says the Lord.*

NEW TESTAMENT verses:

Matthew 18:20 - *For where two or three are gathered together in My name, I am there in the midst of them."*

Matthew 28:19-20 - *Go therefore and make disciples of all the nations, baptizing them in the name of the Father and of the Son and of the Holy Spirit, ²⁰ teaching them to observe all things that I have commanded you; and lo, I am with you always, even to the end of the age." Amen.*

Luke 17:21 - *nor will they say, 'See here!' or 'See there!' For indeed, the kingdom of God is within you."*

John 1:3-5 NKJV - *³ All things were made through Him, and without Him nothing was made that was made. ⁴ In Him was life, and the life was the light of men. ⁵ And the light shines in the darkness, and the darkness did not comprehend it.*

Acts 17:27-28 - *so that they should seek the Lord, in the hope that they might grope for Him and find Him, though He is not far from each one of us; ²⁸ for in Him we live and move and have our being, as also some of your own poets have said, 'For we are also His offspring.'*

Colossians 1:16-17, NKJV - *¹⁶ For by Him all things were created that are in heaven and that are on earth, visible and invisible, whether thrones or dominions or principalities or powers. All things were created through Him and for Him. ¹⁷ And He is before all things, and in Him all things consist.*

3. <u>GOD IS OMNISCIENCE</u>

Omniscience is the property of having complete or maximal knowledge. Along with omnipotence and perfect goodness, it is usually taken to be one of the central divine attributes.

One source of the attribution of omniscience to God derives from the numerous biblical passages that ascribe vast knowledge to him. This is shown in the following biblical (NKJV) verses:

<u>OLD TESTAMENT verses:</u>

1 Chronicles 28:9 - *As for you, my son Solomon, know the God of your father, and serve Him with a loyal heart and with a willing mind;
for the Lord searches all hearts and understands all the intent of the thoughts. If you seek Him, He will be found by you; but if you forsake Him, He will cast you off forever.*

Job 28:24 - *For He looks to the ends of the earth, and sees under the whole heavens.*

Psalms 147:4 - *He counts the number of the stars; He calls them all by name.*

Psalms 127:5 - *Happy is the man who has his quiver full of them; They shall not be ashamed, But shall speak with their enemies in the gate.*

Psalms 147:5 - *Great is our Lord, and mighty in power; His understanding is infinite.*

Isaiah 40:28 - *Have you not known?*
Have you not heard?
The everlasting God, the Lord,
The Creator of the ends of the earth,
Neither faints nor is weary.
His understanding is unsearchable.

Jeremiah 1:5 - *"Before I formed you in the womb I knew you;*
Before you were born I sanctified you;
I ordained you a prophet to the nations."

Jeremiah 23:24 - *Can anyone hide himself in secret places,*
So I shall not see him?" says the Lord;
"Do I not fill heaven and earth?" says the Lord.

Jeremiah 29:11 - *For I know the thoughts that I think toward you, says the Lord, thoughts of peace and not of evil, to give you a future and a hope.*

NEW TESTAMENT verses:

Matthew 9:4 - ⁴ But Jesus, knowing their thoughts, said, "Why do you think evil in your hearts?

Matthew 10:30 - But the very hairs of your head are all numbered.

Matthew 11:27 ²⁷ All things have been delivered to Me by My Father, and no one knows the Son except the Father. Nor does anyone know the Father except the Son, and the one to whom the Son wills to reveal Him.

Matthew 12:25 ²⁵ But Jesus knew their thoughts, and said to them: "Every kingdom divided against itself is brought to desolation, and every city or house divided against itself will not stand.

Acts 1:24 - And they prayed and said, "You, O Lord, who know the hearts of all, show which of these two You have chosen

Romans 11:33-36 - Oh, the depth of the riches both of the wisdom and knowledge of God! How unsearchable are His judgments and His ways past finding out!
³⁴ "For who has known the mind of the Lord?
Or who has become His counsellor?"
³⁵ "Or who has first given to Him
And it shall be repaid to him?"
³⁶ For of Him and through Him and to Him are all things, to whom be glory forever. Amen.

1 Corinthians 2:11 - For what man knows the things of a man except the spirit of the man which is in him? Even so no one knows the things of God except the Spirit of God.

Hebrews 4:13 - *And there is no creature hidden from His sight, but all things are naked and open to the eyes of Him to whom we must give account.*

1 John 3:20 - *For if our heart condemns us, God is greater than our heart, and knows all things.*

4. GOD IS OMNIBENEVOLENCE

The term omnibenevolence means **all-loving**, and the Christian faith teaches that God loves everyone unconditionally and that God is omniscient which means that he is all-knowing. This is shown in the following biblical (NKJV) verses found in the New Testament:

Read:- **John 3:15-21(NKJV)**

1 John 4:1-21 (NKJV),
Love for God and One Another
Knowing God Through Love
Seeing God Through Love
The Consummation of Love
Obedience by Faith

5. THE TRINITY OF GOD

There are over twenty verses within the Holy Bible that describe God as the trinity; that being; God the Father, God the Son and God the Holy Spirit. God is all three, working together in unison, but can also work independently, being part of the Godhead (The Trinity). This is shown in the following biblical (NKJV) verses:

Genesis 1:26 - *²⁶ Then God said, "Let Us make man in Our image, according to Our likeness; let them have dominion over the fish of the sea, over the birds of the air, and over the cattle, over all the earth and over every creeping thing that creeps on the earth."*

Matthew 3:16-17 - *¹⁶ When He had been baptized, Jesus came up immediately from the water; and behold, the heavens were opened to Him, and He saw the Spirit of God descending like a dove and alighting upon Him. ¹⁷ And suddenly a voice came from heaven, saying, "This is My beloved Son, in whom I am well pleased."*

Matthew 28:19 - *¹⁹ Go therefore and make disciples of all the nations, baptizing them in the name of the Father and of the Son and of the Holy Spirit,*

Read **John 1:1-51 (NKJV):** The Eternal Word | The True Light | The Word Becomes Flesh | A Voice in the Wilderness | The Lamb of God | The First Disciples | Philip and Nathanael

Read: ***John 5:1-21 (NKJV):*** Obedience by Faith | The Certainty of God's Witness | Confidence and Compassion in Prayer | Knowing the True—Rejecting the False

John 14:16-17 - *¹⁶ And I will pray the Father, and He will give you another Helper, that He may abide with you forever — ¹⁷ the Spirit of truth, whom the world cannot receive because it neither sees Him nor knows Him; but you know Him, for He dwells with you and will be in you.*

John 14:26 - ²⁶ *But the Helper, the Holy Spirit, whom the Father will send in My name, He will teach you all things, and bring to your remembrance all things that I said to you.*

John 15:26 - ²⁶ *"But when the Helper comes, whom I shall send to you from the Father, the Spirit of truth who proceeds from the Father, He will testify of Me.*

2 Corinthians 13:14 - ¹⁴ *The grace of the Lord Jesus Christ, and the love of God, and the communion of the Holy Spirit be with you all. Amen.*

Philippians 2:5-8 - ⁵ *Let this mind be in you which was also in Christ Jesus,* ⁶ *who, being in the form of God, did not consider it robbery to be equal with God,* ⁷ *but made Himself of no reputation, taking the form of a bondservant, and coming in the likeness of men.* ⁸ *And being found in appearance as a man, He humbled Himself and became obedient to the point of death, even the death of the cross.*

Colossians 1:15-17 - ¹⁵ *He is the image of the invisible God, the firstborn over all creation.* ¹⁶ *For by Him all things were created that are in heaven and that are on earth, visible and invisible, whether thrones or dominions or principalities or powers. All things were created through Him and for Him.* ¹⁷ *And He is before all things, and in Him all things consist.*

Colossians 2:9 - ⁹ *For in Him dwells all the fullness of the Godhead bodily.*

1 Peter 1:2 - ² *elect according to the foreknowledge of God the Father, in sanctification of the Spirit, for obedience and sprinkling of the blood of Jesus Christ: Grace to you and peace be multiplied.*

1 John 5:7-8 *- ⁷For there are three that bear witness in heaven: the Father, the Word, and the Holy Spirit; and these three are one. ⁸And there are three that bear witness on earth: the Spirit, the water, and the blood; and these three agree as one.*

CHAPTER 3

CHRISTIAN PRINCIPLES & VALUES

This Chapter will concentrate on the following two areas:

- **THE CHRISTIAN PRINCIPLES**
- **CHRISTIAN VALUES**

1. **THE CHRISTIAN PRINCIPLES**

The Christian Church has been established through the death and resurrection of Jesus Christ, the Son of God. Jesus Christ is mankind's only redeemer of all sin, and whoever believes in Him and asks for forgiveness for their sins will inherit eternal life.

John 3:16-21 (NKJV) *"For God so loved the world that He gave His only begotten Son, that whoever believes in Him should not perish but have everlasting life. [17] For God did not send His Son into the world to condemn the world, but that the world through Him might be saved.*
[18] "He who believes in Him is not condemned; but he who does not believe is condemned already, because he has not believed in the name of the only begotten Son of God. [19] And this is the condemnation, that the light has come into the world, and men loved darkness rather than light, because their deeds were evil. [20] For everyone practicing evil hates the light and

does not come to the light, lest his deeds should be exposed. ²¹ But he who does the truth comes to the light, that his deeds may be clearly seen, that they have been done in God."

The Old Testament gave testament that God would send His only begotten Son, and the New Testament is testimony that Jesus Christ is the Son of God, who is the Saviour of mankind; for every individual who accepts that He is Our Messiah will inherit eternity with God.

This is clearly evident in the book of **John, chapter 17**, that *"**God had given Him authority over all flesh, that He should give eternal life to as many as You have given Him**"* (**verse 2**).

John 17:1-26 (NKJV), Jesus Prays for Himself | Jesus Prays for His Disciples | Jesus Prays for All Believers

For there is no other way to the living God, but believing and praying upon Jesus Christ, declaring His name, asking for forgiveness for our (individual) sin:

Matthew 6:9-13 (NKJV), The Lord's Pray
⁹ In this manner, therefore, pray:
Our Father in Heaven,
Hallowed be Your name.
¹⁰ Your kingdom come.
Your will be done
On earth as it is in heaven.
¹¹ Give us this day our daily bread.
¹² And forgive us our debts,
As we forgive our debtors.

¹³ *And do not lead us into temptation,*
But deliver us from the evil one.
For Yours is the kingdom and the power and the glory forever. Amen.

Therefore, we must be obedient in following **God's Ten Commandments and Laws**, given not only for the then Israelite nation, but for our own lives within the world.

God's commandments, judgements and laws were written as an instruction on how every man, woman and child should behave in this world (regardless of nationality, race, ethnicity, whether you are Royalty, rich, poor, or slave).

Such laws clearly illustrate God's love for every human, for mankind was created by God, in his likeness, with free will (before falling to sin). This is illustrated in the following:

Deuteronomy 5:6-21 (NKJV), The Ten Commandments
⁶ *'I am the Lord your God who brought you out of the land of Egypt, out of the house of bondage.*
⁷ *'You shall have no other gods before Me.*
⁸ *'You shall not make for yourself a carved image—any likeness of anything that is in heaven above, or that is in the earth beneath, or that is in the water under the earth;* ⁹ *you shall not bow down to them nor serve them. For I, the Lord your God, am a jealous God, visiting the iniquity of the fathers upon the children to the third and fourth generations of those who hate Me,* ¹⁰ *but showing mercy to thousands, to those who love Me and keep My commandments.*
¹¹ *'You shall not take the name of the Lord your God in vain, for the Lord will not hold him guiltless who takes His name in vain.*

¹² 'Observe the Sabbath day, to keep it holy, as the Lord your God commanded you. ¹³ Six days you shall labour and do all your work, ¹⁴ but the seventh day is the Sabbath of the Lord your God. In it you shall do no work: you, nor your son, nor your daughter, nor your male servant, nor your female servant, nor your ox, nor your donkey, nor any of your cattle, nor your stranger who is within your gates, that your male servant and your female servant may rest as well as you. ¹⁵ And remember that you were a slave in the land of Egypt, and the Lord your God brought you out from there by a mighty hand and by an outstretched arm; therefore the Lord your God commanded you to keep the Sabbath day.

¹⁶ 'Honour your father and your mother, as the Lord your God has commanded you, that your days may be long, and that it may be well with you in the land which the Lord your God is giving you.

¹⁷ 'You shall not murder.

¹⁸ 'You shall not commit adultery.

¹⁹ 'You shall not steal.

²⁰ 'You shall not bear false witness against your neighbour.

²¹ 'You shall not covet your neighbour's wife; and you shall not desire your neighbour's house, his field, his male servant, his female servant, his ox, his donkey, or anything that is your neighbour's.'

2. <u>CHRISTIAN VALUES</u>

Please find listed eight Christian Values we should all pertain to in our Christian lives, as Christ taught His disciples and followers. They are:

- **The Father Revealed through Jesus Christ** (the way, the truth, and the life)
- **Love Your Enemies**
- **Patience**
- **Forgiveness and Prayer**
- **Being Like-Minded**
- **Character of the New Man**
- **Kindness**
- **Honourable**

The following contains the Biblical verses to those Christian Values. They are:

a. **The Father Revealed through Jesus Christ**

John 14:6-11 (NKJV): ⁶ *Jesus said to him, "I am the way, the truth, and the life. No one comes to the Father except through Me.*

The Father Revealed
⁷ *"If you had known Me, you would have known My Father also; and from now on you know Him and have seen Him."*
⁸ *Philip said to Him, "Lord, show us the Father, and it is sufficient for us."*
⁹ *Jesus said to him, "Have I been with you so long, and yet you have not known Me, Philip? He who has seen Me has seen the Father; so how can you say, 'Show us the Father'?* ¹⁰ *Do you not believe that I am in the Father, and the Father in Me? The words that I speak to you I do not speak on My own authority; but the Father who dwells in Me does the works.* ¹¹ *Believe Me that I am in the Father and the Father in Me, or else believe Me for the sake of the works themselves.*

Therefore, when you pray, pray to God through Jesus Christ (and no one else), believing that your sins are forgiven by Christ the Son of God (*The Lord's Pray, Matthew 6:9-13, NKJV*).

b. Love Your Enemies

Matthew 5:43-48 (NKJV)
43 "You have heard that it was said, 'You shall love your neighbour and hate your enemy.'
44 But I say to you, love your enemies, bless those who curse you, do good to those who hate you, and pray for those who spitefully use you and persecute you,
45 that you may be sons of your Father in heaven; for He makes His sun rise on the evil and on the good, and sends rain on the just and on the unjust.
46 For if you love those who love you, what reward have you? Do not even the tax collectors do the same?
47 And if you greet your brethren only, what do you do more than others? Do not even the tax collectors do so?
48 Therefore you shall be perfect, just as your Father in heaven is perfect.

c. Patience

James 1:4-6 (NKJV)
4 But let patience have its perfect work, that you may be perfect and complete, lacking nothing.
5 If any of you lacks wisdom, let him ask of God, who gives to all liberally and without reproach, and it will be given to him.
6 But let him ask in faith, with no doubting, for he who doubts is like a wave of the sea driven and tossed by the wind.

d. **Forgiveness and Prayer**

Mark 11:25-26 (NKJV)
25 "And whenever you stand praying, if you have anything against anyone, forgive him, that your Father in heaven may also forgive you your trespasses.
26 But if you do not forgive, neither will your Father in heaven forgive your trespasses."

e. **Being Like-Minded**

Philippians 2:2-8 (NKJV)
2 fulfil my joy by being like-minded, having the same love, being of one accord, of one mind.
3 Let nothing be done through selfish ambition or conceit, but in lowliness of mind let each esteem others better than himself.
4 Let each of you look out not only for his own interests but also for the interests of others.

The Humbled and Exalted Christ
5 Let this mind be in you which was also in Christ Jesus,
6 who, being in the form of God, did not consider it robbery to be equal with God,
7 but made Himself of no reputation, taking the form of a bondservant, and coming in the likeness of men.
8 And being found in appearance as a man, He humbled Himself and became obedient to the point of death, even the death of the cross.

f. **Character of the New Man**

Colossians 3:12-17 (NKJV)
12 Therefore, as the elect of God, holy and beloved, put on tender mercies, kindness, humility, meekness, longsuffering;
13 bearing with one another, and forgiving one another, if anyone has a complaint against another; even as Christ forgave you, so you also must do.
14 But above all these things put on love, which is the bond of perfection.
15 And let the peace of God rule in your hearts, to which also you were called in one body; and be thankful.
16 Let the word of Christ dwell in you richly in all wisdom, teaching and admonishing one another in psalms and hymns and spiritual songs, singing with grace in your hearts to the Lord.
17 And whatever you do in word or deed, do all in the name of the Lord Jesus, giving thanks to God the Father through Him.

g. **Kindness**

Titus 3:4-6 (NKJV)
4 But when the kindness and the love of God our Saviour toward man appeared,
5 not by works of righteousness which we have done, but according to His mercy He saved us, through the washing of regeneration and renewing of the Holy Spirit,
6 whom He poured out on us abundantly through Jesus Christ our Saviour.

Ephesians 4:32 (NKJV)
32 And be kind to one another, tender-hearted, forgiving one another, even as God in Christ forgave you.

h. Honourable

Hebrews 13:4-6 (NKJV)
⁴ Marriage is honourable among all, and the bed undefiled; but fornicators and adulterers God will judge.
⁵ Let your conduct be without covetousness; be content with such things as you have. For He Himself has said, "I will never leave you nor forsake you."
⁶ So we may boldly say:
"The Lord is my helper;
I will not fear.
What can man do to me?"

CHAPTER 4

ESTABLISHMENT OF THE CHRISTIAN CHURCH

1. ESTABLISHMENT OF THE CHRISTIAN CHURCH

It was whilst the apostle Peter was at Joppa that a vision appeared to him from God. The vision illustrated that God's grace and love were not only for believing Jewish Christians but to preach God's Word to all Gentiles so that whoever believes in Jesus Christ, and is baptised will be saved.

Read: *Acts 11:1-18 (NKJV) Peter Defends God's Grace*

Antioch: Disciples called Christians

The Apostles; Barnabas and Paul were at Antioch for a whole year, teaching a great many people, that the name of disciples was first called Christians.

Read: *Acts 11:19-26 (NKJV) Barnabas and Saul at Antioch*

Therefore, through reading the book of Acts we begin to learn of Paul's missionary journeys, teaching God's gospel to Gentile countries (Greece, Macedonia, Turkey, Syria, Crete, Malta and Italy), and their cities.

These four missionary journeys (and companions) were (Read: **Acts** 13-14; 15:39-18:22 (NKJV):

First journey (with Barnabas and Mark, AD 46-48): from Antioch, Salamis, Paphos, Attila, Perga, Iconium, Lystra, Derbe, returning back via Pisidia to Antioch

Second journey (with Silas, AD 49-52): Jerusalem, Caesarea, Ephesus, Corinth, Athens, Berea, Thessalonica, Araphipolis, Philip ol, Neapolis, Troas, Antioch, Iconium, Lystra, Derbe, Tarsus, Antioch, Seleucia

Third journey (AD 53-57): From Antioch, Tarsus, Derbe, Lystra, Iconium, Antioch, Ephesus, Chios, Troas, through Philip ol, Amphipolis, Thessalonica, Berea, Achaia, Corinth, returning via Athens, Berea, Apollonia, Assos, Miletus, Cos, Rhodes, Patara, Tyre, Caesarea and to Jerusalem.

Fourth journey (AD 59-62): from Jerusalem, Sidon, Myra, Caldus, Fair Havens, Malta, Syracuse, Rhegium, Puteoli, Appil Forum, Three Inns and finally Rome.

Paul finally stayed in Rome, being a Roman citizen by birth. It is well documented that the early Christian Church, and Christians, were persecuted within the Roman Empire by the various Caesars.

It is worth noting that in 590AD, Roman Catholicism was developed after Caesar Constantine, by Pope Gregory, the first pope.

Even today, the Roman Catholic Church does not align itself with true Christian beliefs and values, as Christ stated in *John 14:6* *⁶Jesus said to him, "I am the way, the truth, and the life. No one comes to the Father except through Me".*

Therefore, we cannot be reconciled to God through any man or woman born into this world i.e. Pope, Mary – Jesus's mother, etc. as this is a sin, and against God's commandments and laws. We can only be reconciled through the Son of God, Jesus Christ, Our Saviour!

The Bible states that Christ is the Church, **Ephesians 5:22-33 (NKJV)**, therefore why do we seek to create any other denomination(s)?

Ephesians 5:22-33 (NKJV) Marriage—Christ and the Church
²² Wives, submit to your own husbands, as to the Lord. ²³ For the husband is head of the wife, as also Christ is head of the church; and He is the Saviour of the body. ²⁴ Therefore, just as the church is subject to Christ, so let the wives be to their own husbands in everything.
²⁵ Husbands, love your wives, just as Christ also loved the church and gave Himself for her, ²⁶ that He might sanctify and cleanse her with the washing of water by the word, ²⁷ that He might present her to Himself a glorious church, not having spot or wrinkle or any such thing, but that she should be holy and without blemish. ²⁸ So husbands ought to love their own wives as their own bodies; he who loves his wife loves himself. ²⁹ For no one ever hated his own flesh, but nourishes and

cherishes it, just as the Lord does the church. ³⁰ For we are members of His body, of His flesh and of His bones. ³¹ "For this reason a man shall leave his father and mother and be joined to his wife, and the two shall become one flesh." ³² This is a great mystery, but I speak concerning Christ and the church. ³³ Nevertheless let each one of you in particular so love his own wife as himself, and let the wife see that she respects her husband.

For it has become evidence that many good denominational Christian churches have fallen away from the Christian Gospel, preaching their own message and interpretation of God's Word, believing they are doing good, but are causing a great divide to many individuals, as they pursue social, cultural and political acceptance within this world, falling away from Christ truth in not seeking Him first.

It is well known that each Church of England (CoE) and many other churches are not abiding by the commandments of God.

Whilst **Chapter 2 covers God's Commandments**, **Chapter 5** concentrates on those **Judgments and Laws given by God** in the Old and New Testaments. All are still relevant today, as they were from the time God gave instruction(s).

However, there seems to be an increase of elders within the CoE Church; Archbishops, Bishops, Deans, Reverends, Ministers and staff, who have decided not to teach Christ's Gospel with biblical truth and love, within their diocese(s). Their hearts have turned to believing a lie; **Isaiah 5:20 (NKJV)** *²⁰ Woe to those who call evil good, and good evil; Who put darkness for light, and light for darkness; Who put bitter for sweet, and sweet for bitter!*

This has now become the norm for many denominations of Christian Churches, like Uniformed Christian Church, Baptist Church, Methodist Church, Elim Church, Assemblies of God, Bethel Church, Hillsong Church, etc. who are breaking away from traditional Christian beliefs; and are instead introducing non-biblical practices.

2 Timothy 4:1-5
1 "I charge you therefore before God and the Lord Jesus Christ, who will judge the living and the dead at His appearing and His kingdom: ² Preach the word! Be ready in season and out of season. Convince, rebuke, exhort, with all longsuffering and teaching.
3 For the time will come when they will not endure sound doctrine, but according to their own desires, because they have itching ear, they will heap up for themselves teachers; ⁴ and they will turn their ears away from the truth, and be turned aside to fables. ⁵ But you be watchful in all things, endure afflictions, do the work of an evangelist, fulfil your ministry.

The next section considers the Biblical book: the Revelation of Jesus Christ, (given to John on the Island of Patmos), particularly surrounding the letters to the (seven) churches.

2. <u>CORRELATION OF THE (SEVEN) CHURCHES IN REVELATION</u>

The Christian Church has always been persecuted throughout the world because Christians place their faith and love in God's Son, Jesus Christ.

However, there seems to be an increase of persecution happening over many years; where millions of Christians have been persecuted, murdered and killed, tortured and imprisoned, forced to work in hard labour camps, and unable to see their families and friends. Christians are ridiculed by their neighbours, work colleagues, political authorities and even within their own families.

Matthew 24:1-2 (NKJV) Jesus Predicts the Destruction of the Temple
24 Then Jesus went out and departed from the temple, and His disciples came up to show Him the buildings of the temple. ² And Jesus said to them, "Do you not see all these things? Assuredly, I say to you, not one stone shall be left here upon another, that shall not be thrown down."

Matthew 24:3-14 (NKJV) The Signs of the Times and the End of the Age
³ Now as He sat on the Mount of Olives, the disciples came to Him privately, saying, "Tell us, when will these things be? And what will be the sign of Your coming, and of the end of the age?"
⁴ And Jesus answered and said to them: "Take heed that no one deceives you. ⁵ For many will come in My name, saying, 'I am the Christ,' and will deceive many. ⁶ And you will hear of wars and rumours of wars. See that you are not troubled; for all these things must come to pass, but the end is not yet. ⁷ For nation will rise against nation, and kingdom against kingdom. And there will be famines, pestilences, and earthquakes in various places. ⁸ All these are the beginning of sorrows.
⁹ "Then they will deliver you up to tribulation and kill you, and you will be hated by all nations for My name's sake. ¹⁰ And then many will be offended, will betray one another, and will hate one another. ¹¹ Then many

false prophets will rise up and deceive many. ^{12} *And because lawlessness will abound, the love of many will grow cold.* ^{13} *But he who endures to the end shall be saved.* ^{14} *And this gospel of the kingdom will be preached in all the world as a witness to all the nations, and then the end will come.*

There seems to be a correlation between those seven churches as indicated in the book of **Revelation chapters 1, 2 & 3** (Ephesus, Smyrna, Pergamos, Thyatira, Sardis, Philadelphia, and Laodiceans), and the events happening throughout the world today:

Revelation 1:4-20 (NKJV) - Greeting the Seven Churches
^{4} *John, to the seven churches which are in Asia:*
Grace to you and peace from Him who is and who was and who is to come, and from the seven Spirits who are before His throne, ^{5} *and from Jesus Christ, the faithful witness, the firstborn from the dead, and the ruler over the kings of the earth.*
To Him who loved us and washed us from our sins in His own blood, ^{6} *and has made us kings and priests to His God and Father, to Him be glory and dominion forever and ever. Amen.*
^{7} *Behold, He is coming with clouds, and every eye will see Him, even they who pierced Him. And all the tribes of the earth will mourn because of Him. Even so, Amen.*
^{8} *"I am the Alpha and the Omega, the Beginning and the End," says the Lord, "who is and who was and who is to come, the Almighty."*

Vision of the Son of Man
^{9} *I, John, both your brother and companion in the tribulation and kingdom and patience of Jesus Christ, was on the island that is called Patmos for the word of God and for the testimony of Jesus Christ.* ^{10} *I was in the Spirit on the Lord's Day, and I heard behind me a loud voice, as of*

a trumpet, [11] saying, "I am the Alpha and the Omega, the First and the Last," and, "What you see, write in a book and send it to the seven churches which are in Asia: to Ephesus, to Smyrna, to Pergamos, to Thyatira, to Sardis, to Philadelphia, and to Laodicea."
[12] Then I turned to see the voice that spoke with me. And having turned I saw seven golden lampstands, [13] and in the midst of the seven lampstands One like the Son of Man, clothed with a garment down to the feet and girded about the chest with a golden band. [14] His head and hair were white like wool, as white as snow, and His eyes like a flame of fire; [15] His feet were like fine brass, as if refined in a furnace, and His voice as the sound of many waters; [16] He had in His right hand seven stars, out of His mouth went a sharp two-edged sword, and His countenance was like the sun shining in its strength. [17] And when I saw Him, I fell at His feet as dead. But He laid His right hand on me, saying to me, "Do not be afraid; I am the First and the Last. [18] I am He who lives, and was dead, and behold, I am alive forevermore. Amen. And I have the keys of Hades and of Death. [19] Write the things which you have seen, and the things which are, and the things which will take place after this. [20] The mystery of the seven stars which you saw in My right hand, and the seven golden lampstands: The seven stars are the angels of the seven churches, and the seven lampstands which you saw are the seven churches.

It is not God's intention to condemn the seven churches or the world, but to show His Love and Compassion, so they/ we redeem themselves back to Him, through focusing and believing upon His Son, Our Saviour Jesus Christ.

Read:
Revelation: Chapters 2 & 3 - The Seven Churches:
Revelation 2:1-7 (NKJV) The Loveless Church, "Ephesus"

Revelation 2:8-11 (NKJV) The Persecuted Church, "Smyrna"
Revelation 2:12-17 (NKJV) The Compromising Church, "Pergamos"
Revelation 2:18-29 (NKJV) The Corrupt Church, "Thyatira"
Revelation 3:1-6 (NKJV) The Dead Church, "Sardis"
Revelation 3:7-13 (NKJV) The Faithful Church, "Philadelphia"
Revelation 3:14-22 (NKJV) The Lukewarm Church, "Laodiceans"

Therefore, it is essential that the Christian Church does not follow or align itself with evil or perverse practices as stated by Jesus Christ in Revelation.

CHAPTER 5

THE DECLINE OF CHRISTIAN VALUES AND MORALS

This Chapter has been written to enable the reader to understand those established Christian values and morals; given by God, for the whole of mankind.

It is clear that Christian morals have slowly been eroded; nationally, internationally and globally, to such an extent that evil has been portrayed as good, in the eyes of The Church of England, the UK and Global Governments and Monarchy, the Political Parties and Leaders, Financial Institutions, Banks and Global Markets, The Health Service, the Environment, etc.

Isaiah 5:20-23 (NKJV)
[20] *Woe to those who call evil good, and good evil;*
Who put darkness for light, and light for darkness;
Who put bitter for sweet, and sweet for bitter!
[21] *Woe to those who are wise in their own eyes,*
And prudent in their own sight!
[22] *Woe to men mighty at drinking wine,*
Woe to men valiant for mixing intoxicating drink,
[23] *Who justify the wicked for a bribe,*
And take away justice from the righteous man!

God has already ordained the times and events, where all nations, churches and people will turn against (and away) Him, believing and following sin.

This is shown in the books of the Old and New Testaments, **Holy Bible (NKJV)**:

God's Laws and Judgments are still relevant in the World

Most Relevant Verses	
The Old Testament	
Verse	**Laws and Judgements**
Exodus 20:13	You shall not murder.
Exodus 35:2	"For six days work may be done, but on the seventh day you shall have a holy day, a sabbath of complete rest to the Lord; whoever does any work on it shall be put to death.
Leviticus 11:10-12	But whatever is in the seas and in the rivers that does not have fins and scales among all the teeming life of the water, and among all the living creatures that are in the water, they are detestable things to you, and they shall be abhorrent to you; you may not eat of their flesh, and their carcasses you shall detest. Whatever in the water does not have fins and scales is abhorrent to you.
Leviticus 11:13	These, moreover, you shall detest among the birds; they are abhorrent, not to be eaten: the eagle and the vulture and the buzzard.
Leviticus 11:20	All the winged insects that walk on all fours are detestable to you.

Leviticus 11:23	But all other winged insects which are four-footed are detestable to you.
Leviticus 11:41	'Now every swarming thing that swarms on the earth is detestable, not to be eaten.
Leviticus 11:42	Whatever crawls on its belly, and whatever walks on all fours, whatever has many feet, in respect to every swarming thing that swarms on the earth, you shall not eat them, for they are detestable.
Leviticus 18:22	You shall not lie with a male as one lies with a female; it is an abomination.
Leviticus 18:29	For whoever does any of these abominations, those persons who do so shall be cut off from among their people.
Leviticus 20:13	If there is a man who lies with a male as those who lie with a woman, both of them have committed a detestable act; they shall surely be put to death. Their blood guiltiness is upon them.
Leviticus 20:14	If there is a man who marries a woman and her mother, it is immorality; both he and they shall be burned with fire, so that there will be no immorality in your midst.
Deuteronomy 7:25-26	The graven images of their gods you are to burn with fire; you shall not covet the silver or the gold that is on them, nor take it for yourselves, or you will be snared by it, for it is an abomination to the Lord your God. You shall not bring an abomination into your house, and like it come under the ban; you shall utterly detest it and you shall utterly abhor it, for it is something banned.

Deuteronomy 12:31	You shall not behave thus toward the Lord your God, for every abominable act which the Lord hates they have done for their gods; for they even burn their sons and daughters in the fire to their gods.
Deuteronomy 18:12	For whoever does these things is detestable to the Lord; and because of these detestable things the Lord your God will drive them out before you.
Deuteronomy 22:5	A woman shall not wear anything that pertains to a man, nor shall a man put on a woman's garment, for all who do so are an abomination to the Lord your God.
Deuteronomy 22:23-24	"If there is a girl who is a virgin engaged to a man, and another man finds her in the city and lies with her, then you shall bring them both out to the gate of that city and you shall stone them to death; the girl, because she did not cry out in the city, and the man, because he has violated his neighbour's wife. Thus you shall purge the evil from among you.
Deuteronomy 24:1-4	"When a man takes a wife and marries her, and it happens that she finds no favour in his eyes because he has found some indecency in her, and he writes her a certificate of divorce and puts it in her hand and sends her out from his house, and she leaves his house and goes and becomes another man's wife, and if the latter husband turns against her and writes her a certificate of divorce and puts it in her hand and sends her out of his house, or if the latter husband dies who took her to be his wife (read more).

Deuteronomy 25:13-16	"You shall not have in your bag differing weights, a large and a small. You shall not have in your house differing measures, a large and a small. You shall have a full and just weight; you shall have a full and just measure, that your days may be prolonged in the land which the Lord your God gives you (read more).
Deuteronomy 25:16	For everyone who does these things, everyone who acts unjustly is an abomination to the Lord your God.
Deuteronomy 27:15	'Cursed is the man who makes an idol or a molten image, an abomination to the Lord, the work of the hands of the craftsman, and sets it up in secret.' And all the people shall answer and say, 'Amen.'
Proverbs 3:32	For the devious are an abomination to the Lord;
	But He is intimate with the upright.
Proverbs 6:16-19	There are six things which the Lord hates,
	Yes, seven which are an abomination to Him:
	Haughty eyes, a lying tongue,
	And hands that shed innocent blood,
	A heart that devises wicked plans,
	Feet that run rapidly to evil,
	A false witness who utters lies,
	And one who spreads strife among brothers.
Proverbs 8:13	The fear of the Lord is to hate evil;
	Pride and arrogance and the evil way
	And the perverted mouth, I hate.
Proverbs 11:1	A false balance is an abomination to the Lord,

	But a just weight is His delight.
Proverbs 11:20	The perverse in heart are an abomination to the Lord,
	But the blameless in their walk are His delight.
Proverbs 12:22	Lying lips are an abomination to the Lord,
	But those who deal faithfully are His delight.
Proverbs 13:19	Desire realized is sweet to the soul,
	But it is an abomination to fools to turn away from evil.
Proverbs 15:8	The sacrifice of the wicked is an abomination to the Lord,
	But the prayer of the upright is His delight.
Proverbs 16:5	Everyone who is proud in heart is an abomination to the Lord;
	Assuredly, he will not be unpunished.
Proverbs 17:15	He who justifies the wicked and he who condemns the righteous,
	Both of them alike are an abomination to the Lord.
Proverbs 20:10	Differing weights and differing measures,
	Both of them are abominable to the Lord.
Proverbs 24:9	The devising of folly is sin,
	And the scoffer is an abomination to men.
Proverbs 28:9	He who turns away his ear from listening to the law,
	Even his prayer is an abomination.
Proverbs 29:27	An unjust man is abominable to the righteous,
	And he who is upright in the way is abominable to the wicked.
Jeremiah 32:34	But they put their detestable things in the house which is called by My name, to defile it.

Ezekiel 8:6	And He said to me, "Son of man, do you see what they are doing, the great abominations which the house of Israel are committing here, so that I would be far from My sanctuary? But yet you will see still greater abominations."
Ezekiel 22:11	One has committed abomination with his neighbour's wife and another has lewdly defiled his daughter-in-law. And another in you has humbled his sister, his father's daughter.
Daniel 12:11	From the time that the regular sacrifice is abolished and the abomination of desolation is set up, there will be 1,290 days.
Daniel 9:27	And he will make a firm covenant with the many for one week, but in the middle of the week he will put a stop to sacrifice and grain offering; and on the wing of abominations will come one who makes desolate, even until a complete destruction, one that is decreed, is poured out on the one who makes desolate."
The New Testament	
Verse	**Laws and Judgements**
Matthew 24:15	"Therefore when you see the abomination of desolation which was spoken of through Daniel the prophet, standing in the holy place (let the reader understand)".
Mark 7:20-23	And He was saying, "That which proceeds out of the man, that is what defiles the man. For from within, out of the heart of men, proceed the evil thoughts, fornications, thefts, murders, adulteries, deeds of

	coveting and wickedness, as well as deceit, sensuality, envy, slander, pride and foolishness.
Mark 13:14	"But when you see the abomination of desolation standing where it should not be (let the reader understand), then those who are in Judea must flee to the mountains.
Luke 16:15	And He said to them, "You are those who justify yourselves in the sight of men, but God knows your hearts; for that which is highly esteemed among men is detestable in the sight of God.
Romans 1:18-32	*The Guilt of Mankind*
	18 For the wrath of God is revealed from heaven against all ungodliness and unrighteousness of men, who suppress the truth in unrighteousness, 19 because what may be known of God is manifest in them, for God has shown it to them. 20 For since the creation of the world His invisible attributes are clearly seen, being understood by the things that are made, even His eternal power and Godhead, so that they are without excuse, 21 because, although they knew God, they did not glorify Him as God, nor were thankful, but became futile in their thoughts, and their foolish hearts were darkened. 22 Professing to be wise, they became fools, 23 and changed the glory of the incorruptible God into an image made like corruptible man-- and birds and four-footed animals and creeping things. 24 Therefore God also gave them up to uncleanness, in the lusts of their

	hearts, to dishonour their bodies among themselves, 25 who exchanged the truth of God for the lie, and worshiped and served the creature rather than the Creator, who is blessed forever. Amen. 26 For this reason God gave them up to vile passions. For even their women exchanged the natural use for what is against nature. 27 Likewise also the men, leaving the natural use of the woman, burned in their lust for one another, men with men committing what is shameful, and receiving in themselves the penalty of their error which was due. 28 And even as they did not like to retain God in their knowledge, God gave them over to a debased mind, to do those things which are not fitting; 29 being filled with all unrighteousness, sexual immorality, wickedness, covetousness, maliciousness; full of envy, murder, strife, deceit, evil-mindedness; they are whisperers, 30 backbiters, haters of God, violent, proud, boasters, inventors of evil things, disobedient to parents, 31 undiscerning, untrustworthy, unloving, unforgiving, unmerciful; 32 who, knowing the righteous judgment of God, that those who practice such things are deserving of death, not only do the same but also approve of those who practice them.
1 Corinthians 6:9	Or do you not know that the unrighteous will not inherit the kingdom of God? Do not be deceived; neither fornicators, nor

	idolaters, nor adulterers, nor effeminate, nor homosexuals,
Galatians 3:23-25	But before faith came, we were kept in custody under the law, being shut up to the faith which was later to be revealed. Therefore the Law has become our tutor to lead us to Christ, so that we may be justified by faith. But now that faith has come, we are no longer under a tutor.
Revelation 21:8	But for the cowardly and unbelieving and abominable and murderers and immoral persons and sorcerers and idolaters and all liars, their part will be in the lake that burns with fire and brimstone, which is the second death."
Revelation 21:27	and nothing unclean, and no one who practices abomination and lying, shall ever come into it, but only those whose names are written in the Lamb's book of life.

1 Timothy 4:1-4 (NKJV) **The Great Apostasy**

4 Now the Spirit expressly says that in latter times some will depart from the faith, giving heed to deceiving spirits and doctrines of demons, ² speaking lies in hypocrisy, having their own conscience seared with a hot iron, ³ forbidding to marry, and commanding to abstain from foods which God created to be received with thanksgiving by those who believe and know the truth. ⁴ For every creature of God is good, and nothing is to be refused if it is received with thanksgiving;

2 Timothy 3:1-7 (NKJV) **Perilous Times and Perilous Men**

3 But know this, that in the last days perilous times will come:

² *For men will be lovers of themselves, lovers of money, boasters, proud, blasphemers, disobedient to parents, unthankful, unholy,*
³ *unloving, unforgiving, slanderers, without self-control, brutal, despisers of good,*
⁴ *traitors, headstrong, haughty, lovers of pleasure rather than lovers of God,*
⁵ *having a form of godliness but denying its power. And from such people turn away!*
⁶ *For of this sort are those who creep into households and make captives of gullible women loaded down with sins, led away by various lusts,*
⁷ *always learning and never able to come to the knowledge of the truth.*

As you can tell from reading the above verses, particularly 2 Timothy verse 3-7, the world (including the United Kingdom) has already turned their hearts away, and against God.

But did you not realise that God already knew this! God has already determined a time that this world will be destroyed, and that at the time of Christ return to judge the world, those who believe in Him will be saved, to be granted eternal life with him on a new sinless World. Those who do not believe will live in eternal darkness (Hades/ Hell), with Satan and the fallen angels (demons). This is predicted in:

Read:-
Romans 2:1-16 (NKJV) - God's Righteous Judgment
Revelation 19:1-21 (NKJV) - Heaven Exults over Babylon | Christ on a White Horse | The Beast and His Armies Defeated

1. THE CHURCH OF ENGLAND

a. What is Truth

"Come out from them and be separate, says the Lord. Touch no unclean thing ... and I will be a Father to you, and you will be My sons and daughters..."
2 Corinthians 6:17-18 (NKJV)

Anglican bishops apparently think the answer to Pilate's knotty question goes something along the lines, 'Truth is a multi-faceted interpretation of reality that evolves and changes over time according to cultural revision.' Whether their belief is that God changes, or that transformation stems from our own advancing perception, is a moot point – as perhaps is whether some of them actually believe in God or not. But the end result is the same. The majority appear to have become moral and doctrinal relativists, with Scripture no longer regarded as a revelation of the immutable Word of God, but rather a Self-affirming 'manual', dependent for interpretation on ideologically driven, and necessarily transient, cultural identity.

God made everything and everyone the way they are, the thinking appears to go, so everything is good, and let no man condemn the 'truth' of another.

Such an approach is misconceived, replacing worship of God with worship of Self. Notwithstanding, in pursuit of their quest to drag Christianity into this utopian world of Neverland – where mankind has in theory come of age and anything goes – the bishops in February 2023, debated prayers and services of blessing for same-sex couples, currently denied full marriage in church. This, they argued, will preserve the unity of the Church, by on the one hand upholding traditional teaching on marriage, and the other extending love and affirmation to those who, over the centuries, have suffered cruel persecution simply for being 'who they are'.

It is clearly right that as a Church we repent any failure to love and care for those who come seeking help. We are all sinners, and Christ loves all equally – it was precisely to save sinners that He came. But the bishops would do well to remember that, while we are told to love sinners, we are commanded at the same time to reject sin, and that the Bible unequivocally prohibits all sexual relations outside marriage. It also clearly labels as sin, without exception, adultery, fornication, homosexuality, incest and bestiality. But perhaps most worrying of all, it tells us that if we persist in sin and refuse to repent, we shall be excluded from God's Kingdom. As summed up by Paul in his letter to the Galatians, *'I do not set aside the grace of God; for if righteousness comes through the law, then Christ died in vain.'* (**Galatians 2:21, NKJV**).

Of course, this doesn't mean that God 'hates' sinners. Let us repeat, God loves us so much that He sent His own Son into the world to set us free. But the perhaps uncomfortable truth is that goodness and evil cannot co-exist. It's simply impossible, and in this life, we have to choose one side or the other. When we choose to follow Christ, we don't overnight become perfect, of course – and there will unquestionably be times when we fall again into sin. But as we repent, the Holy Spirit comes alongside us, to strengthen and help … to ready us for heaven.

When we willingly persist in sin, we cut ourselves off from that help and from a chance of restoration. From being whole. Effectively, we write our own judgement. This is why the bishops' attempt to reconfigure what constitutes sin is so reprehensible, because, in the light of eternity, it denies help to those caught in sin. Thereby, the Church fails in its duty of care.

To say you will uphold the traditional teaching of the Bible on marriage as a union between one man and one woman for life, and then offer services of prayer and blessing for same-sex couples, is hypocrisy. However, dressed up, such a stance is a formal reclassification of same-sex relationships as approved by God and of equal standing with heterosexual union between one man and one woman. It is not a demonstration of God's love, but a bowing to pressure on the part of those who would change the fundamental tenets of Christianity into a revived form of paganism, that has at its heart sexual licence and Self.

Similarly, and whatever campaigners may claim, the drive to use gender-neutral terms when referring to God and to develop in general 'more inclusive language', is not at heart designed to enrich the Christian faith, but is rather a weapon wielded by the liberal elite in their battle to destroy patriarchy and the religious underpinnings of Western culture (https://www.theguardian.com/world/2023/feb/07/church-of-england-to-consider-use-of-gender-neutral-terms-for-god).

If adopted, such a move can only further and fatally weaken the Church, called by God to guard the truth and care for believers.

The Christian Church must urge the bishops to genuinely uphold Christian doctrine and exercise, before it's too late, proper pastoral oversight of those, committed by God, to their care. Let the Church once again become the Church of God, and not merely a lapdog Church of England, compromised by woke aspirations to overturn the values and beliefs that have given strength and stability to our society for well over a thousand years.

Should, however, they persist in such stubborn and perfidious betrayal of the faith, it is surely time for believers to have the courage robustly to defend Biblical truth, and to distance themselves from so-called 'liberalising' attempts to undermine and reconfigure Christian belief.

Source: Voice for Justice UK, 2022/ 23

b. Defining Love - Archbishops of Canterbury & York (The Church of England)

If, when faced with Jesus, Pontius Pilate famously posed the question, 'What is truth?', we can perhaps justifiably ask today, 'What is love?'.

Is it the unquestioning affirmation of life-style choices that have led to social fragmentation and a breakdown of order? That have left literally millions of lonely individuals incapable of forming committed and lasting relationships, and with spiralling rates of mental illness and addiction problems affecting both young and old alike (https://researchbriefings.files.parliament.uk/documents/SN06988/SN06988.pdf)?

Or is it the defence of Christian values and traditional morality, which – though admittedly dismissed by many as outmoded – have, down the centuries, provided order and stability for both individuals and society and kept us strong?

Somewhat perversely, it may be thought – given its divinely appointed charge to uphold the faith and protect the flock – the Church of England appears to take the former view. In its report, *Love Matters*, commissioned by the Archbishops of Canterbury and York and published in April 2023, it aims to put forward a vision of the future based on what it calls 'love-in-action' (https://www.churchofengland.org/sites/default/files/2023-04/H%26F%20report%20DIGITAL%20SINGLE%20PAGES.pdf).

Focussing on families and households, the report's expressed aim is to be inclusive and more accepting of diversity – in fact, it doesn't just want to 'accept' but to celebrate diversity, recognising and affirming the legitimacy of all committed couple relationships, whether married, unmarried, in a civil partnership, opposite or same-sex… and everything in between. The report says it wants to see a more forgiving, kinder, and fairer society.

As might be expected, given the background to the report, much is made of the Christian call to unconditional love. Citing Paul, the report's authors define love as 'not envious, boastful, arrogant or rude … not irritable or resentful'. Rather, they say, love is patient and kind, putting up with all things. And they conclude, '(Love) is a commitment to give to – and promote the flourishing of – another person'. All of which is undeniably true, but the trouble is that at heart this is a policy document for social action. It is political. The call to honour God and obey His commands, as set down in the Bible – which is the essence of Christian belief – is not just absent, but denied. In particular, the exclusive monogamous union of one man and one woman in marriage for life is set aside as irrelevant. It is a life-long commitment that must be supported, the report says, and marriage may well be seen as desirable for achieving this end, but it is not of primary concern.

Harsh though it may sound, this is giving support to the belief system of a new religion – and that religion is, at the core, hostile not just to Christianity, but to human flourishing and life. It is a doctrine that not just leaves people damaged and unhappy, but that denies them all possibility of redemption, because it locks them into sin, with no chance of escape. Endorsing the transient satisfaction of what men and women *think* they want, but which leaves them with only the ashes of broken dreams, is not love. It's not even close. It's a manifesto for oppression.

Is it really for this that our Saviour went head-to-head with Satan in that terrible struggle on the Cross? Is this the freedom for which He died?

Since that decisive battle two thousand years ago, the devil has fought might and main to reassert his hold. He can't ultimately win, of course, as he knows only too well. It is beyond question that the Lord will return in glory after every man, woman and child on the planet has been given the chance to hear the good news and repent, and so be saved. But during this time of dispensation, while judgment is delayed, Satan still holds power and his will, as ever, is to subvert and destroy. The call of the Church is to take the message of salvation out into the world, to be a light in the darkness and to uphold truth, while guarding the flock against attack.

It is time for the Archbishops of Canterbury and York to recognise which side they are truly on. That of God, or of the devil. It must be one or the other. But it can't be both.

Source: Voice for Justice UK, 2022/ 23

c. Another chip in the wall

In a recent survey conducted by the disingenuously named Campaign for Equal Marriage in the Church of England, it was announced by the chairman of the group that over 1100 licensed priests in the Anglican Church say they will be happy to conduct same-sex marriages, if and when they become legal (https://www.churchtimes.co.uk/articles/2022/28-october/news/uk/we-will-conduct-same-sex-marriages-say-more-than-1000-clergy).

He reportedly enthused, "It is clear from the feedback after *Living in Love and Faith* that the majority want the current situation to change."

Given that the Church of England says there are currently around 18,000 active clergy in the UK (https://www.churchofengland.org/sites/default/files/2020-06/Ministry%20Statistics%202019%20report%20FINAL.pdf).

It is challenging to see how he can assert this with such seeming confidence; but, notwithstanding, the survey is interesting. For instance, one wonders why, when those surveyed appear to hold so cavalier approach to Scripture and Christian doctrine, they are in holy orders in the first place. Exactly what is this faith they so energetically follow? Because as sure as God made little apples, it's not Christianity! And by what logic do they now claim the right to rewrite our faith to make it more culturally relevant?

A few basics:
(1) Christ died on the Cross to break Satan's hold and set us free from sin, so that we might be restored to that relationship with God for which we had been created.
(2) From the dawn of creation, marriage was God's gift to Adam, because God had seen that by himself the man was lonely.

To find for him therefore a fitting companion, Eve was created from Adam's own rib, so that together the man and the women would complement and complete each other. From the beginning, therefore, the union of the man and the woman was both gift and sacrament, binding them together for the period of their lives, in exclusive and monogamous union, so that they might support and care for each other, and together care for any children that might result.

Our urban warriors masquerading as priests, however, appear intent on denying these fundamental pillars of our faith, rehabilitating 'sin' so as to present it as 'good' and thereby negating at source the need for Christ's sacrifice. In fact, Jesus is relegated to the role of rather wishy-washy good example, proclaiming eternal love without judgment, and who would doubtless, if He'd thought about it at all, have fervently embraced LGBT inclusivity and gender choice.

Let us not be deceived. This is apostasy, and a gospel of despair that can serve only to root people in error and separate them yet further from God. Those who argue differently are not fit to care for the people of God. They should be ashamed.

Source: Voice for Justice UK, 2022/ 23

d. **Apostasy – the abandonment or renunciation of a religious or political belief or principle**

The Church of England announced in January 2022 that Stephen Knott is to be the new Archbishop's Appointment Secretary. No, this does not mean that he will be overseeing Justin Welby's diary – as, from the job title, one might be excused for imagining. Rather this is one of the most senior appointments in the Anglican Church, carrying responsibility for the appointment of bishops, deans, and other senior posts in the Church of England, and involving close collaboration with the Prime Minister's Appointments Secretary (https://www.archbishopofcanterbury.org/news/news-and-statements/stephen-knott-be-new-archbishops-secretary-appointments).

In fact, it can with justification be said that whoever is appointed to this task holds the key to all future appointments in the Church of England and the direction that it takes.

What is of primary significance in Mr Knott's appointment, however – albeit unmentioned in the official announcement – is that he is 'married' to Major General Alastair Bruce of Crionaich, Governor of Edinburgh Castle. The pair were apparently married in July last year in St John's Episcopal Church, Edinburgh, with the ceremony conducted by no less a personage than the Rt Revd John Armes, Bishop of Edinburgh (https://virtueonline.org/lambeth-deputy-become-archbishops-appointment-secretary-married-homosexual).

From his clear commitment to the social normalisation of same-sex relationships, it is to be expected that Mr Knott's recommendations will support the promotion of greater 'diversity and inclusivity'. His appointment is, therefore, a clear challenge to those who uphold traditional doctrine as set down in the Bible and, whether intended or not, is a laying down of battle lines.

While asserting God's love for all, the website for the Anglican Communion states unequivocally that homosexual practice is incompatible with Scripture. It stands on the commitment of the Church to 'uphold faithfulness in marriage between a man and a woman in lifelong union'. It further states that abstinence is right for those who are not called to marriage' (https://www.anglican communion.org/resources/document-library/lambeth-conference/1998/section-i-called-to-full-humanity/section-i10-human-sexuality).

Yet, in sanctioning the appointment of Mr Knott – a man who is not just same-sex attracted but in a 'marriage' celebrated in direct contravention of existing guidelines – it would appear that Justin Welby has chosen to override the clear doctrinal position of the Church of which he is the de facto leader, preferring to promote so-called diversity. By this one action he has nailed his colours firmly to the mast of secular inclusivity, and betrayed his oath of obedience to the teachings of the Church.

Mr Knott is free to follow whatever life-style he so desires, but the choices he has made disbar him from holding office in the Christian Church. By making this appointment, therefore, the Church of England proclaims that it is apostate and that it has rejected the clear teachings of Christ. It says it is no longer the Church of God – but, truly, a Church of England. Those who believe in the Bible can no longer, with integrity, follow these warped and blasphemous teachings, that make a mockery of Christ's sacrifice on the Cross.

Source: Voice for Justice UK, 2022/ 23

e. **The one and only King**

Based on what they describe as 'a landmark survey' of frontline Anglican clergy carried out by themselves, The Times newspaper claims that three-quarters of Church of England priests believe that Britain can no longer be described as a Christian country, and view with unease the increasing decline in Church attendance. In an effort to reverse the trend, The Times claims that the majority of clergy now want to bring Christianity more into line with public opinion by conducting same-sex weddings and dropping the Church's traditional opposition to premarital and gay sex (https://www.thetimes.co.uk/article/church-of-england-christianity-survey-gay-marriage-sex-female-archbishop-70ck07sj6).

To conduct the survey, The Times contacted a total of 5,000 names, selected at random from Crockfords Clerical Directory of Anglican Clergy, out of which 1,200 chose to respond. As well as calling for a radical overhaul of Church doctrine, many of the respondents also apparently reported high levels of stress, even claiming to be at breaking point, and with almost a third saying that they had considered quitting in the last five years.

One cannot help but feel, if they really are so intent on changing The Church's historic doctrine, that it might be better if they had, because, whatever faith they now espouse, as sure as God made little apples, it's not Christianity. From their calls for change, it would seem indeed as if the wolves have got in amongst the sheep, and our misguided clerics are no longer acting as guardians of the flock, but have rather become agents of subversion – spokespersons for a new religion, that has at its heart not obedience to God, but worship of 'Self'.

This then truly is a survey of the Church of England, wedded, as it appears, to upholding and celebrating contemporary culture. But let's be honest, it's a religion founded, not on Christ, but on secularism ... and to this extent it is demonic. In this belief system, man is acclaimed as the centre of the universe, architect and determiner of moral value, with the power to control and even re-orchestrate the building blocks of life. So, God is dismissed as an illusion before what is claimed the reality of humanism – perhaps the greatest delusion of all.

Such a religion deserves to die. But Christianity will not be so easily discarded, because, whatever the claims of respondents to the survey, it is founded on Truth, and speaks to a higher good. Christianity alone rescues men and women from the miasma and contagion of what is, at the end of the day, sin. Christianity alone sets us free, allowing us to become fully what God has made, and intends us, to be.

The "Voice for Justice UK" is conducting its own survey in 2023/24, directed at discovering the extent to which Christians are free to manifest and practise their belief in modern society. They have so far received over 1,500 responses – far higher, it will be noted, than those collected by The Times, and responses are still coming in. Full assessment of the data will not, of course, be carried out until the survey closes, but preliminary analysis already suggests a very different picture from that presented by The Times. In particular, we have had a large number of responses from grassroots Christians under the age of 35, 90% of whom, far from wanting a more liberal approach to faith, are strong in upholding traditional, Bible-based belief.

So, does this reflect a declining Church? Or does it rather indicate a resurgence of belief, as handed down by the apostles?

Perhaps more to the point, however, in relation to implied claims by The Times that Christianity, if it's to survive, needs to become more 'relevant' to modern society, when asked about their freedom to express Christian belief in public, a surprising number of respondents of all ages have reported pressure to conform to secular dogma not just in work and social settings, but from within their local church, where staff teams, headed by clergy, appear to be pushing for change.

Two questions therefore occur. First, is the apparent decline in Church attendance a result of society's loss of interest, or rather the result of an unacceptable watering down of faith? And second, is the pressure to align Christian belief with popular opinion part of a focussed campaign by those whose primary allegiance is not to God, but rather to the Woke values of society?

Yes, the survey by The Times is very important ... not because it shows the state of Christian faith in the UK today, but because it reveals the extent to which Anglican clergy have become infected with the contagion of secular liberalism. Indeed, it is arguable that our far larger survey promises to show more clearly the true state of faith in Britain today – and what has been revealed so far indicates not a call for closer alignment with populist woke values, but a vibrant and growing community of believers, dedicated to upholding the teachings of Christ in a compromised and increasingly hostile secular world.

Source: Voice for Justice UK, 2022/ 23

f. Living in so-called 'love'. But not faith.

In a surprise announcement in October 2023, Church of England bishops declared that prayers of blessing for same-sex couples – based on recommended prayers and readings included in the highly controversial *Prayers of Love and Faith* report – should be commended for use and now go forward for authorisation under Canon law. It is expected that the process, involving consultation with every diocese, will take until 2025.

This follows a fulsome public apology by the bishops earlier this year to LGBTQI+ people, for the way in which they said the Church had in the past rejected or excluded them. "We have not loved you as God loves you," the apology read, "and that is profoundly wrong.

This would seem to reflect a growing trend in popular culture to misidentify the condemnation of actions that the Bible regards as sinful as hatred for sinners themselves. Such an interpretation could not be further from the truth. To condemn 'sin', which can only damage the individual by tying them into oppressive and harmful behaviours, is an expression of love at its most profound, because only in and by such condemnation is there any possibility of liberation and healing – of restoration to that fulness of being that is the birth-right and gift of God to all. As it is, rebranding what the Bible labels 'sin' as virtue makes a mockery of Christ's sacrifice, binding the sinner to suffering and eternal death.

Let us be clear, Christ died to set us free from sin and to give us life. In His own body, Jesus bore the price for our rebellion, dying in our place, so that when we confess our sins, we are healed by His blood. When, therefore, the bishops say that what the Bible labels as 'sin' is *good*, they not just make a mockery of that sacrifice – they deny any possibility of liberation and healing. They turn the gospel, in fact, into a mandate for demonic oppression.

We are none of us perfect, but, thankfully, our salvation is not dependent on sinlessness – only on our acknowledgment of sin and repentance, and our obedience to Christ. It is this chance of salvation that the bishops now deny, becoming spokespersons for a toothless and time-serving church that seeks to serve not God, but an immoral State, dominated as it by woke values of liberal conformity.

It is true that, since the announcement, eleven bishops have come forward to say that they believe the collective decision of the House of bishops is wrong, but the disappointing reason they give is that it fails to safeguard the pastoral stability, mission and unity of the Church (https://www.premierchristianity.com/uk-church/exclusive-dissenting-bishops-speak-out-on-same-sex-blessings/16497.article).

Their stance would have carried more weight had they simply said that the decision lacked spiritual integrity and was theologically wrong. As instance of which, they could have cited the statement of the Bishop of London, Sarah Mullaly, who co-chaired the steering group for the report and announced, as justification, "… the heart of the gospel is reconciliation – our desire is to remain together as one Church in our uncertainty, finding ways to live well with our different perspectives and convictions" (https://www.churchofengland.org/media-and-news/press-releases/prayers-love-and-faith-bishops-agree-next-steps-bring-synod).

At every level, she is wrong. The *heart of the gospel* is the love of God, made manifest in the death and resurrection of His Son, Jesus Christ, who in His own body bore the penalty for sin and died that we might live.

The *heart of the gospel* is God's love for the lost and our redemption.

It is not, as the bishop asserts, reconciliation with transient cultural views founded on adult sexual preferences, committed, amongst other things, to normalising and promoting behaviours that until recently were classified as deviant. That are still, according to the Bible, sin. This is what the dissenting bishops should have said, and this is the message the world still needs to hear.

As it is, the wolves have got in amongst the flock and are causing mayhem. But, despite appearances, God has not abandoned His Church and He calls to believers, "Come out from them and be separate ... Touch no unclean thing, and I will receive you ... I will be a Father to you, and you will be my sons and daughters" (**2 Cor 6: 17 -18**).

Source: Voice for Justice UK, 2022/ 23

g. Sound the alarm – the wolves have got in amongst the flock

On 15 November, the General Synod of the Church of England narrowly approved a motion to allow a trial for standalone services of blessing for same sex couples. The move follows a decision by Synod last February to push forward with full implementation of Prayers of Love and Faith, a resource designed for use with same sex couples seeking Christian recognition and blessing for their union (https://www.christiantoday.com/article/more.divided.than.the.conservative.party/141054.htm).

Predictably, the move has sparked major controversy. Although the services will not be formal weddings, they will include the exchange of rings, prayers, confetti, and a blessing by the officiating priest. In other words, a service of marriage in all but name. Mindful of dissent, however, Synod has been quick to reassure those not 100% on board that the new service will be introduced only 'on a trial bases,' after which, in 2025, there will be further discussion as to whether or not the measure be formally adopted. A two thirds majority will then be required for full authorisation (https://www.churchofengland.org/media-and-news/

press-releases/synod-backs-trial-special-services-asking-gods-blessing-same-sex).

What sophistry is this! Under canon law, given time for presentation to Parliament and full debate, authorisation for such services would normally take around two years. By calling for a 'trial period' ahead of ratification, however, the delay becomes circumvented, allowing services to go ahead immediately. Telling us that this is to allow opportunity for assessment of their full impact and effect on the wider communion is misleading, and appears deliberately deceptive. It doesn't need to be pointed out, for example, that once such services have been allowed to take place in supportive parishes, it will be well-nigh impossible at a later date to reverse the process.

But quite apart from any distaste felt for such underhand manipulation of canon law – designed, as it is, to safeguard the faith – infinitely worse is the harm being caused to the Church. A community that appears so casually to jettison doctrine can no longer be regarded as a fit custodian of the faith. It has, in fact, become salt that has lost its flavour, and is fit only to be thrown away.

We are all sinners, and thank the Lord He doesn't require us to be perfect before we become part of His Church, but that does not mean that we can in any way, shape or form affirm what, according to the Bible, is sin. The cardinal point of Christianity is that Christ *saves us from sin*. It follows that, once we accept Him as Lord, it becomes the work of the Spirit to heal and transform us in our inmost parts, conforming us to the image of Christ – making us fit for heaven. It is a work that continues throughout our lives while we remain on earth.

Beyond that, scripture is clear that marriage between one man and one woman, in exclusive and monogamous union for the period of their natural lives, is the gift of God, given for our mutual support in a fallen world, and so that the couple together may raise and care for any children that result. It is equally clear that all sex outside marriage is prohibited, for the simple reason that it damages that bond – and which, it goes without saying, includes pre-marital sex, adultery, same sex relations, incest and bestiality.

But now wolves, who reject and attempt to redefine Scripture in their adoration of Self, have got in amongst the flock, and the shepherds are seemingly nowhere in sight. Indeed, it is wolves who have now taken on the mantle of the shepherds, and they are wreaking devastation, leading many astray by their unholy and perverse doctrines.

The question must surely be asked, on what basis can those who so casually deny the authority of Scripture presume to call themselves Christian? And on what basis can they presume to wield authority?

The new faith, so stridently defending 'love' in all its forms, makes mockery of Christ's sacrifice on the Cross. And, in the process, it denies to sinners the chance of redemption, and of healing – of becoming fully what the Lord has made, and intends them, to be.

It is time for the true shepherds to stand up and defend the flock. The wolves must not just be thwarted in their attempt to assert power – for the protection and wellbeing of the sheep, they must be cast out.

Source: Voice for Justice UK, 2022/ 23

2. <u>POLITICAL, CULTURAL AND SOCIAL PRESSURE, ACCEPTANCE AND INFLUENCES</u>

a. Faith in our time – let the fight back begin (Secular, liberal and the permissive society)

We live in an increasingly secular, supposedly 'liberal' and permissive society, which is another way of saying 'anything goes!' In the midst of all this, the call of the Church is to be light and truth, and to act as a moral compass. Over the last years, however, the Church has abandoned this role, *adapting* the message of salvation to fit more comfortably with what activists would have us believe is compassionate tolerance and acceptance of all.

After all, the argument runs, would a loving God (if He actually exists) have made people to be the way they are, if He hadn't intended them to be that way? And despite what it says about God's creating men and women in His own image, it's obvious that some people are born in the wrong body, i.e. that God got their gender wrong. So, it's pretty obvious that the Bible is simply a product of its time, and its moral imperatives are, therefore, essentially wrong. Or (version 2) we've interpreted it wrongly and it's time to update it to the 21st century.

A major problem for Christians in countering these essentially duplicitous arguments is that we have allowed activists, intent on changing society, to frame the narrative. We have accepted almost without question that we are intolerant, judgmental bigots, and have been so fearful of causing offence that we have gone along with their insistence that men and women have an absolute right to do whatever feels good, whenever and wherever they want – because this is being true to themselves, the universal and ultimate determinant of being.

Which actually means that believers too have bowed down before the great god Self. Maybe from the best of motives – they want to show love and be tolerant, as commanded by Christ – but the net result is that they concede vital ground. Even worse, trying to straddle an extremely uncomfortable fence, our vacillating apologists discover they're no longer sure what it is they really do believe. So the wheel comes full circle, and they start to try and redefine their faith in order to make it fit.

Let us be clear, the reframing of Christianity to make it 'more' relevant to the prevailing culture is apostasy. Such an approach makes mockery of Christ's sacrifice and binds the unwary to chaos, putting them once again under bondage to sin. Whether we understand it or not, this is a direct challenge by Satan to God.

The secularists, of course, think they've got things sewn up. This God – this fairy in the sky, as some mockingly call Him – hasn't done anything yet, and it's a pretty safe bet He won't. Christians are delusional! Small wonder they think they're winning! But actually, this is a very dangerous position to take. God does see all, and He will respond. This time of supposed non-response is not indicative of a failure to react – proving His non-existence – but is rather allowing a period of grace, giving as many men and women as possible a chance to repent and be saved ... before the inevitable comes.

But come it will.

Increasing and unmanageable debt, financial turmoil, scandal after scandal and political chaos, corruption, growing authoritarian control, collapse of the nation's infrastructure (seen most clearly in the NHS) ... and over all the growing threat of war. Let us make no mistake, these are first rumblings of the approaching storm, which will be like nothing ever before seen.

The only hope of surviving what is to come is to repent. The truth is, God loves us so much that He sent His only begotten Son, Jesus Christ, into the world to save us from sin (**John 3:16, NKJV**). That battle was fought and won at the Cross, and those of us who acknowledge Christ as Lord have been set free and restored to that relationship with God for which we were created. However, that salvation – freely given – demands choice. We cannot hover around the middle, trying to hedge our bets. It is a conflict between life and death, and we all have to choose which side we are on.

For the future of the human race, it is imperative that Christians stand up for the faith and honour God. We must stop being so apologetic and reclaim the narrative, upholding without compromise the values of the Bible and our allegiance to Christ.

All of life is the gift of God, and the marriage of one man and one woman for life in exclusive and monogamous union, for their mutual support and the bringing up of any children they might have, was given by God at our creation for the wellbeing and survival of humanity. All sexual relations outside marriage are prohibited: because they weaken that exclusive union, cause harm to the individuals involved, put at risk the wellbeing of any children that might be conceived, and damage the wider community. Same sex 'marriage' is therefore, by definition, forbidden, as is co-habitation of any kind.

Similarly, the destruction of life before birth through the exercise of maternal and/or paternal 'choice' is sin. Deliberately ending the life of another before their allotted time is also sin. Suggesting to children that they are born 'in the wrong body' and can choose what they want to be by mutilating intervention … is sin.

Andrew Bridgen's Bill in Parliament (June 2023) to ban the promotion of gender transitioning in schools was narrowly defeated by 40 votes to 34 (https://www.dailymail.co.uk/news/article-12239043/Bid-ban-social-gender-transitioning-schools-narrowly-killed-MPs.html#:~:text=A%20bid%20to%20ban%20the,his%20proposals%20for%20new%20laws).
Out of 650 MPs, only 74 cared enough to turn out to vote, and the majority voted **against** protecting children from this dangerous ideology now being peddled in schools, and ruining so many lives. The bottom line is, we are normalising and promoting mental illness, and we are imposing such ideas onto young children, who, by definition, cannot judge the validity of what they are being taught for themselves.

Shame on those MPs! And shame on us – that we have allowed this poisonous and dangerous teaching to take root and spread. Where are the leaders of the Church? Why are they not crying out against this abuse? Where are grassroot Christians? Why are we not barricading the gates of Parliament and demanding protection for our children?

It is time for Christians to recover our voice, that we might best defend those who cannot defend themselves ... and indeed everyone. The future of humanity is at stake.

Source: Voice for Justice UK, 2022/ 23

b. Woke Branding – a challenge to God

As part of the current delusional euphoria that marks the rebranding of gender identity, it would seem that women are being airbrushed out of existence. How else to account for the extraordinary decisions by Budweiser, Nike, and now Adidas, to use a biological male – in process of transition, it's true, but still very definitely male – to promote their products?

By convoluted mental gymnastics, Budweiser's decision is perhaps just possibly understandable ... though not justifiable. Sales figures for their American style lager have apparently over recent months dipped significantly, so enlisting the offices of transwoman influencer and TikTok personality Dylan Mulvaney was no doubt a misguided attempt to rebrand themselves as inclusive and appealing to all. Funky ... ahead of the game! If that was the reasoning, however, the attempt has been a spectacular failure – in fact, a marketing disaster, because, since the advert appeared, enraged consumers have boycotted the brand and sales have plummeted even further (https://www.washington examiner.com/news/bud-light-dylan-mulvaney-business-sales-down).

But with regards Nike and Adidas, the decision to use a transwoman to promote respectively a sports bra and a women's swimsuit is wholly incomprehensible. For their advert, Nike once again used Dylan Mulvaney, who apparently has the breasts of a 'thirteen year old' as result of hormone therapy, but is still awaiting surgery to complete the transitioning process (https://www.express.co.uk/comment/expresscomment/1756225/nike-dylan-mulvaney-trans-bra-advert). Good for him! It should be pointed out, however, that men do not wear bras. And, even with hormone fuelled AA size breasts, by no stretch of the imagination does Dylan Mulvaney qualify to advertise sports bras to women who really do require support.

For their advert, however, Adidas has scaled even greater heights, because the model they have used is so obviously male, it almost beggars belief (https://www.dailymail.co.uk/news/article-12098975/Calls-boycott-Adidas-womens-swimwear-advert.html). Its new women's swimwear line is apparently part of its Pride collection, listed as gender-neutral and backed by no less a personage that Tom Daley. This in itself feels rather surreal, but even given the company's backing for inclusivity, how can they possibly justify using a model, *for a woman's swimsuit*, who is so clearly a man? Who stands 6'2" in his bare feet, has a flat, hairy chest – with no attempt at concealment – and a very obviously bulging crotch?

The expression 'having a laugh' comes to mind, but this isn't even remotely funny. Rather, it's tragic, because it says that biological women don't matter – that the distinctives of what is to be a woman are, in fact, irrelevant. After all, if a man can call himself a woman, invade female only spaces, participate in women's sports, and even demand women's healthcare - that, by definition, can't apply to a man - what does it say about the nature and worth of women?

For over two thousand years, women have had to fight hard to gain recognition as independent beings of worth, with God-given strengths and talents that were always intended by our Creator for use. To be more, in fact, than mere reproductive machines, wholly dependent on men, with the sole task of bringing up children and keeping house. The promotion of gender choice makes mockery of both that battle and women's achievements. And it perpetuates the notion of female inferiority, because it says that both the nature and biology of women are irrelevant. Instead, 'woman' becomes merely pouty lips, makeup, hair, big breasts, and 4" stilettos.

At every level this is wrong. The Bible is clear in laying down the pattern for our creation as male and female, together and jointly reflecting the image of God. More, in Eve's creation from Adam's rib, it spells out that the man and the women complement and complete each other. We are not, and are not made to be, the same. Rather, the sexes have distinctive characteristics that define both our natures and calling in this life. Women, by virtue of the fact they give birth, are more nurturing and empathetic; men, primarily tasked with providing for the family, are 'hunter-gatherers' and territorial.

This is not to say that men and women don't share certain characteristics. It is undeniable that both sexes are equally capable of tenderness and of aggression. But women tend to be physically smaller and are not as strong and, while the impulse of men is to guard their territory, theirs, commonly, is to create a home that will provide safety for the family. It is these God-given distinctives that are both violated and denied by today's aggressive insistence that gender is choice, and that you can have whatever reality you want – be whatever you want – simply by declaring it as truth.

Let us make no mistake, at heart this trend towards woke advertising is a demonic attack on the creation of men and women as made in the image of God, and encouraging the delusion can only exacerbate the chaos already engulfing society. It is part of the same challenge to God that was first made by the serpent in Eden. Now, as then, the aim is to confuse, delude ... and ultimately destroy.

Source: Voice for Justice UK, 2022/ 23

c. Transgender Movement

As transgender activists become ever more strident, it would seem that the fight back has at last begun in earnest. Allowing biological men to take over women's sport was always deeply problematic, and British Cycling's new policy to allow only those born female to compete in women's races is to be welcomed. Yet it has provoked a howl of outrage, surely out of all proportion to its perfectly reasonable defence of women's rights. After all, it goes without saying that those born biologically male will in general be taller and stronger than their female counterparts, and if, on top of that, they have undergone puberty, they will retain a performance advantage that no amount of hormone suppressant will ever totally remove (https://www.bbc.co.uk/sport/cycling/65718748).

That said, in recent years there appears to have been a definite trend for some male athletes to transition and then carry on competing in female-only events. And unsurprisingly, in many of these events they have wiped the board. Trans swimming star Lia Thomas, for example, last year (2022) controversially won the US National Collegiate Athletic Association (NCAA), America's top trophy in university sports. Thomas subsequently robustly denied allegations of unfair performance advantage, but it is a fact that at 6'1" this biological male towered over fellow competitors and was physically stronger, with a far greater 'wingspan'(https://heightline. com/lia-thomas-height-how-tall-is-the-swimmer-and-what-is-his-current-weight/).

Similarly, Fallon Fox, the American former MMA martial arts champion, continued post-transition to compete in contests, but only against women, and famously broke the skull of one of her opponents (https://www.sportskeeda.com/mma/news-when-transgender-fighter-fallon-fox-broke-opponent-s-skull-mma-fight).

Perhaps unsurprisingly, fellow American Ronda Rousey subsequently refused to fight Fox, because she said, "I feel like if you go through puberty as a man it's something that you can't really reverse. You can't just reverse that, there's no undo button on that" (https://www.thepinknews.com/2014/09/20/martial-arts-champ-refuses-to-take-on-transgender-fighter-fallon-fox/).

The advantage given by male body-type seems so blindingly obvious, the statement feels almost oxymoronic. A point reinforced by British Cycling, which, as justification for its new policy, stated, "Research studies indicate that even with the suppression of testosterone, transgender women who transition post-puberty retain a performance advantage …".

Trans-cyclist Emily Bridges, however, was quick to dismiss such justification as mere politically motivated opposition to transgender inclusion. In a statement to the BBC, in the article referenced above, she said, '… discussion of the debate is "inherently political" and "framed by the media who are driven through engagement by hate".' She further added she was "terrified to exist", and that British Cycling was, "… furthering a genocide against us," ominously ending, "Bans from sport is how it starts".

So, in Emily Bridges' view, it would seem that anyone who doesn't accept without qualification transgender demands and upholds science is a perpetrator of genocide. Charming. It would seem that free-speech is great, but only so long as it upholds the chosen narrative.

As long overdue signs of fight back begin to emerge, sadly, the scale of the battle appears to be increasing. The unpleasant truth would seem to be that trans activists are intent on having their own way at whatever cost, with absolutely no interest in the rights of others. Thus, the rights of both real women and children are casually dismissed – sacrificed on the altar of imposed choice, with biological sex either treated with contempt or dismissed as illusion.

At heart, this is a battle to reconfigure society, not just by destroying traditional moral values and family, but by challenging our individual creation – as fearfully and wonderfully made, male and female, in the image of God. It is the about the re-allocation of control by imposition of a distorted version of reality that, if allowed, will annihilate world culture, and the tactics employed to achieve this are further distortion and intimidation. This was clearly illustrated at a recent rally in Hyde Park organised by 'Let Women Speak', where a masked group of trans rights protestors rallied behind banners calling for trans kids to be armed, alongside an image of a play car carrying a machine gun (https://www.telegraph.co.uk/news/2023/05/28/let-women-speak-transgender-activists-protest-hyde-park/). They also carried banners proclaiming, "Terfs off our turf, defending trans lives." The clear message overall was, 'Don't mess with us, or you'll regret it!'

It goes without saying, especially today, that some people are confused about their gender and need both help and support, but this is a far-bigger battle than affirmation of the gender dysphoric. This is a war without quarter, and it is the future of humanity that is at stake. It is manifestation of the age-old conflict between God and the devil. Whatever the pressure, in order to preserve our humanity, it is a battle we must win.

Source: Voice for Justice UK, 2022/ 23

d. Why is Costa celebrating harmful trans mastectomies?

The death was reported in the press in early August 2023 of Russian social media influencer Zhanna Samsonova. The name may mean little to you, but Ms Samsonova had apparently gained fame for blogging about her extreme diet of raw tropical fruit. She died, aged 39, of malnutrition (https://www.telegraph.co.uk/world-news/2023/08/01/zhanna-samsonova-tiktok-instagram-vegan-diet-dies/).

What, you may ask, has this got to do with Costa's advertisement of an androgynous looking cartoon character, with blue hair, yellow shorts, a cup of coffee ... and mastectomy scars? Well, the answer is simple – some behaviours should not be affirmed, because of the harm they cause. And Costa's advert is a case in point.

Costa claims as justification for its advertisement that it is promoting inclusivity and diversity. A spokesperson for the chain said, "At Costa Coffee, we celebrate the diversity of our customers, team members and partners ... We want everyone that interacts with us to experience the inclusive environment that we create, to encourage people to feel welcomed, free and unashamedly proud to be themselves (https://www.independent.co.uk/news/uk/home-news/costa-coffee-trans-man-mural-b2385455.html)." The image was apparently taken from part of a mural created in Brighton for last year's Pride month.

Seriously?

In the last few years, the number of children seeking treatment for gender dysphoria has sky rocketed, going from 250 in in 2011/12, to over 5,000 in 2021/22. A decade ago, the majority of referrals were for birth-registered males, but more recently that has been reversed, with far higher numbers of birth-registered females now seeking treatment in their early teens. Significantly, a very high proportion of children claiming to be suffering from gender incongruence, of both sexes, have mental health problems or are autistic (https://www.england.nhs.uk/commissioning/spec-services/npc-crg/gender-dysphoria-clinical-programme/implementing-advice-from-the-cass-review/).

If transitioning treatment genuinely did resolve all problems, one might possibly – just possibly – be able to say the advert was fine and that there was no cause for concern, but there is increasing evidence that it does not. Suicidal tendencies among transgender people following treatment remain far higher than among the general population, with between 32% to 50% attempting suicide at least once (https://www.ncbi.nlm.nih.gov/pmc/articles/ PMC 5178031/).

Similarly, rates of mental illness remain far higher, with 58% of transgender patients having at least one psychiatric diagnosis (https://www.ncbi.nlm.nih.gov/pmc/articles/PMC6830528/), as compared with 25% among non-transitioners (https://www.mind.org.uk/media-a/2958/statistics-facts-2017.pdf). On top of that, though precise numbers still have to be determined due to the difficulties in accessing accurate information, we know that there are growing numbers of trans individuals who subsequently deeply regret their choices and actively seek help to detransition (https://www.bmj.com/content/381/bmj-2022-073584; https://news.sky.com/story/hundreds-of-young-trans-people-seeking-help-to-return-to-original-sex-11827740).

All of these are what could be called 'adverse outcomes' to gender transitioning treatment. Yet it might perhaps be said that as they only affect some – even if that 'some' is actually more than half – what does it matter? Well, it 'matters' because there are other outcomes, following medical and surgical intervention, that affect all trans people, ranging from infertility and difficulties relating to sexual arousal, to the lifelong need for medication, and a long list of possible health problems, such as, for example, blood clots and osteoporosis.

Put all these together, and it's no exaggeration to say that the efficacy of such treatment is at best problematic and, at worst, downright dangerous. The question has then to be asked: why would anyone with a grain of common sense seek to 'glorify' such unnecessary and hazardous bodily mutilation?

Costa is clearly on the woke bandwagon and intent on banging the drum, but encouraging vulnerable young girls to mutilate their otherwise healthy bodies is not just irresponsible, but abuse of the worst kind. Cutting off their breasts is not cool – as suggested by the advert – but rather medical masochism, which in the future there is every likelihood they will deeply regret. As said at the beginning, some behaviours should not be affirmed because of the harm they cause.

Costa claim they want to be inclusive and celebrate diversity, but exactly who are they 'including' here? Not women, clearly. And not those suffering from breast cancer, for whom the advert shows deep insensitivity. No, their claimed diversity is both selective and exclusionary. They should be ashamed.

Source: Voice for Justice UK, 2022/ 23

e. **Dodgy diversity schemes – No thanks!**

Pogrom – a mob attack, approved or condoned by authorities, against the persons and property of a religious, racial or national minority (htttps://www.britannica.com/topic/pogrom).

In an extremely welcome and, some might think, long overdue move recognising the reality of Stonewall's underhand campaign to impose LGBT ideology on the rest of society, the Government has at long last issued guidance telling all government departments to withdraw from the gay rights' group controversial and mis-named 'Diversity scheme' (https://www.dailymail.co.uk/news/article-10549173/Now-Whitehall -told-ditch-Stonewall-amid-row-charitys-divisive-diversity-scheme.html).

At last, a glimmer of sanity!

Let us be clear, nobody is suggesting that we now support discrimination against LGBTQ people because of their sexual orientation - but this is precisely what Stonewall's pernicious diversity programme has attempted to do, demanding that everyone sign up to and support their version of repressive equality and inclusivity. Rarely can the word 'equality' have been so misused, because in the Stonewall version of reality, anyone not buying into their pogrom of moral redefinition has been subjected to discrimination, harassment, vilification, exclusion – and even criminalisation! And Bible-believing Christians especially have been the target of denunciation, because of the prohibition in Scripture against all sex outside marriage between one man and one woman, in exclusive and monogamous union for life. In Stonewall's world, no one is allowed to say this, because it's evidence of outdated bigotry and religious intolerance and all such views must be rigorously suppressed.

All of which, one would have thought, makes Stonewall's version of diversity an oxymoron – a clear contradiction in terms. Of even greater concern, however, is the fact that the so-called diversity programme has become a weapon for indoctrination, even imposing acceptance of LGBT ideology onto children, in a deliberate attempt to reconfigure society.

In the 19th century, Karl Marx identified schooling as a tool for transmitting class or group ideology. It is a lesson LGBTQ+ activists have learned well, demanding that children from age 3 onwards be taught that they can choose their gender, that LGBT relations are exactly the same as heterosexual relations, and that all 'families' are the same. This is brain-washing on an industrial scale, and that Government departments are now recognising the political motivations underlying so called diversity schemes is welcome indeed.

Yet the Government now needs to go much further. In particular, it must recognise that the deliberate and targeted marginalisation of Christians is, at heart, manifestation of a secularist drive to re-orchestrate our values and so smash the building blocks that have provided the foundations of our society and made us strong for over a thousand years.

In multicultural, multi-faith Britain, over the last couple of decades we have expended vast amounts of time and money attempting to enforce "diversity", and make society more sexually and racially accommodating to people and views that were once alien or little known. In some ways this has been good, yet now our historic and easy-going tolerance, and readiness to welcome and help those in need, is being exploited against us. Our once proud history, for example, is being relabelled colonialism and exploitative supremacy, our 'heroes' vilified, and our young taught to be ashamed of their heritage and 'colour'. Meekly accepting, we have all become complicit in orchestrating 'suppression' of the majority, and the result is our society overall has become morally decadent, corrupt, and weak.

Justice cannot be reduced to a matter of competition between different 'groups', and the debate should not be about rewriting our history, so as to emphasise perceived wrong by a minority group. Rather the focus should be on what we have done right, so that we might build on that and move forward together. It is surely then time to reconsider who we are, and rediscover and affirm the historic Christian values on which our society is founded.

Since February 2022, the world has witnessed the violent and unprovoked invasion of Ukraine by Russia, with President Putin, under the fiction of protecting national security and 'liberation', swearing to annihilate Ukrainian independence. This puts not just Ukraine, but the whole of the rest of the world, in jeopardy, and it is no exaggeration to say that the West now faces a challenge not seen since the Second World War. In such a conflict, Russia will pay no heed to our rebranded values and woke protestations of fairness.

The perhaps unpalatable truth is that unless we recover our strength, and take a stand on the real values underpinning society, we shall fall. Let us then reaffirm our commitment to genuine justice and truth, that we may effectively aid those under attack and stand against the real evils now threatening us and the rest of the world.

Source: Voice for Justice UK, 2022/ 23

f. **The triumph of ideology over reason**

A new report by the highly respected and influential think tank Policy Exchange has found that 40% of state secondary schools allow children to self-declare their gender without parental consent or knowledge. The report, based on more than 300 freedom of information requests made to a randomly selected group of schools, found that four in ten operated policies of gender self-ID, with a massive three quarters failing to inform parents of their child's gender "distress". At the same time, it found that schools dealing with a "gender-distressed" child required staff and other pupils to affirm the child's new identity. It also found that at least 19 per cent of secondary schools were failing to maintain single-sex changing rooms or cloakroom facilities, meaning that vulnerable adolescent girls, whatever their personal views, were being forced to share what should be their 'safe' spaces with males (https://policyexchange.org.uk/publication/asleep-at-the-wheel/).

The Report's findings reveal not just the shocking extent to which schools have become compliant with radical gender ideology – the belief that masculine and feminine distinctions are at base social constructs that operate to maintain outmoded cultural dominance – but also their rampant failure to safeguard the children in their care, as required under law. This is unacceptable. The unconscionable truth is that children of all ages, and as young as five, are being routinely taught that a person's gender identity may be different from his or her biological sex, and that some people are "born in the wrong body". Small wonder the number of children presenting as gender dysphoric has skyrocketed in recent years!

It is surely time for us to face the truth. Without socially engineered pressure, the numbers involved are actually extremely small – according to recent figures released by the Office for National Statistics, the number of people identifying as trans was 262,000 people, or 0.5% of the population (https://www.ons.gov.uk/peoplepopulationandcommunity/culturalidentity/genderidentity/bulletins/genderidentityenglandandwales/census2021).

The current trend is not towards enlightenment and compassionate recognition for vast numbers of people, cruelly and wrongfully oppressed by outmoded religion, or even exploitative capitalism endangered by challenge to the status quo. It is political indoctrination of the worst kind, by ideologues whose sole purpose, it would seem, is to destroy the moral framework of society.

Let us be clear, the purpose of education is to equip and prepare a child for adult life, giving them the skills that will enable them to take their place in, and contribute to, society. It goes without saying that no two children are the same, and one of the primary functions of education must be to help a child identify and best develop their own unique gifts, allowing them to discover 'who' and 'what' they are, without pressure and within a safe environment.

It is neither the function nor objective of education to attempt to control or direct the ideas and values by which an individual chooses to live, or to demand social conformity with a disputed value system for which there is no scientific or biological base.

At the same time, schools are required by law to remain politically impartial, which means that the promotion of partisan political views – such as gender ideology – is prohibited and that, where political issues are taught, there should be a balanced presentation of opposing views (https://www.gov.uk/government/publications/political-impartiality-in-schools/political-impartiality-in-schools).

In recent years, however, this has gone by the board, with *beliefs* about gender identity becoming embedded within the curriculum as though they are facts, and opposing or dissenting views – even those legitimately based on religion – rigorously suppressed.

Our schools' system, that was once the envy of the world, has become not just inadequate but, to quote the Policy Exchange's own assessment, 'rotten to the core'.

Allowing overtly LGBT campaign groups, such as Stonewall or Mermaids, to shape educational policy, in the process embedding their controversial and highly disputed beliefs about gender identity, is not just a recipe for disaster, but is a dereliction of the duty we owe our young.

Children are the future and this insanity must end. In particular, the ideological promotion of gender choice, for which there is no scientific basis, must be removed from education, and parents must be informed of any issues their child might be having. And they, not schools or even social services, must be allowed to decide what constitutes their child's best help and support. Similarly, current social coercion that puts teachers in fear for their jobs if they fail to comply with the new Weltanschauung must end, as must the coercive intimidation of all who disagree on religious grounds.

Source: Voice for Justice UK, 2022/ 23

g. Light in the darkness

When a society loses its way and becomes decadent, it dies. From the beginning of history, we have seen this time and again, most famously perhaps with the fall of the Roman Empire. The usual, and perhaps most straightforward, reason given is that it became overstretched and suffered a string of military defeats in its encounters with barbarian tribes, combined with a loss of centralised political control that was to prove fatal. All of which is most assuredly true, but its decline was unquestionably exacerbated by the moral decay, degeneracy and general weakness that became a hallmark of Roman society in its latter years.

The same traits – seen in the unremitting focus on Self and demand for instant gratification – are perhaps evident in our own society today. It's not so much that moral standards have slipped, as that we are rapidly losing the values on which our society is founded and has up to now flourished. Even worse perhaps, in this brave new world of reconfigured morality, we demand that 'old' values, such as sexual purity, faithfulness and the requirement of commitment, be proscribed, with those who dare give voice to such reactionary notions branded intolerant bigots, and even criminalized.

As instance of this, in the news this week we have had the story of Izzy Montagu, a Christian mother now suing her 4 year old son's Primary school for forcing him to take part in a Pride parade (https://www.dailymail.co.uk/news/article-11702239/Christian-mother-sues-four-year-old-sons-school-saying-LGBT-parade.html).
Her request for the boy to be excused, because the event went against the family's Christian beliefs, was apparently summarily dismissed. Even worse, it was treated with contempt, because at a meeting Izzy attended at the school to discuss the matter, the head teacher's daughter wore a t-shirt saying, 'Why be racist, sexist, homophobic or transphobic, when you can just be quiet?' Needless to say, at that same meeting, Izzy's request was turned down.

This is unacceptable. Have we really reached the point where anyone who upholds traditional faith can simply to be bludgeoned into silence? Because this is what was going on here.

Article 9 of the European Convention on Human Rights, as enforced under UK law in the Human Rights Act 1998 states, 'Everyone has the right to freedom of thought, conscience and religion ... either alone or in community with others and in public or private, to manifest his religion or belief, in worship, teaching, practice and observance' (https://www.legislation.gov.uk/uk pga/1998/42/schedule/1/part/I/chapter/8).

However, Heavers Farm Primary, intent on enforcing its ideological message of 'equality', apparently felt it could ignore this.

This is bigotry and discrimination of the worst kind, and must be called out and exposed for what it is. It is surely time for activists to be held to account.

Source: Voice for Justice UK, 2022/ 23

h. "... we shall make the West so corrupt; it stinks." (Willi Münzenberg)

It would appear that this prediction by Willi Münzenberg, German communist and one of the founders of the now infamous Frankfurt School, is reaching fulfilment.

To take a recent example, according to a recent report in The Times, most schools, including some leading independent schools such as Wellington and Brighton College, have now adopted gender-neutral uniform policies. The aim, it is claimed, is to allow children to wear clothes that "most reflect their self-identified gender" (https://www.thetimes.co.uk/article/skirting-the-issue-school-uniform-names-go-gender-neutral-pmkbqp7tw).

How thoughtful, I hear you say – but what's Willi Münzenberg got to do with this? The answer is simple – if, to many, unpalatable. Normalising and promoting gender choice for vulnerable children, by definition exploring who and what they are and their place in the world, can only heighten their confusion and further intensify the climate of moral ambivalence that has been steadily growing in the West. An ambivalence that is direct result of the focused attack on our civilisation, first orchestrated by Bolshevik intellectuals in the early part of the last century, as they attempted to impose Communism across Europe and the wider world.

Let's be honest, such a policy has nothing to do with child safeguarding and protection. Rather, it is the promotion and normalisation within society of adult sexual preferences and orientations by LGBTQ activists – which behaviours were, until very recently, labelled perversion. In short, what we are seeing is the latest manifestation of a covert endeavour to bring about regime change, on this occasion through the manipulation of children. Who lack the necessary intellectual and emotional development both to assess the validity of what they are being taught and to defend themselves.

But back to the Frankfurt School, because the policies put forward then are directly relevant to the situation with which we find ourselves faced today. In the immediate aftermath of the 1917 revolution in Russia, the Bolsheviks had confidently expected that Communism would spread throughout the rest of Europe. But, to their shock, this didn't happen, so Lenin, by that point firmly established as the head of government, set up what was called an Institute of Social Research to find out why.

Comprised of Marxist intellectuals, the group rapidly identified as the main problem the Judaeo-Christian legacy, which they said was underpinning Western Society, giving not just structure and form, but hope and purpose to 'the common man'. To pave the way for global Socialist revolution, therefore, they devised a complex psychological strategy aimed at bringing about complete destruction of the values and institutions on which Western society rested, targeting specifically the family, which they saw as one of the main building blocks for society ... and religion.

It was a strategy specifically designed to produce mass hopelessness and alienation, destroying faith in God and any idea of transcendent purpose that might provide some sort of unifying force for society as a whole. Their ideas, however, didn't find universal approbation and Stalin, when he came to power, expelled the group for being too extreme. Hence the groups removal in 1923 to Frankfurt ... where they continued their diabolical work. As part of this, and in order to facilitate social psychosis and enable control, they advocated such things as the teaching of sex and homosexuality to children; mass provision of contraceptives to school children; breakdown and destabilisation of the family; promotion of mass immigration to destroy national identity; control and manipulation of the media; destabilisation of the legal system; and the dependency of all individuals on the state. All of which they aimed to bring about by the exploitation of what Lenin had previously branded 'useful idiots' – influential people susceptible to persuasion, who would be encouraged to endlessly question the system and, on the back of that, promote ideas that would foment chaos and ultimate collapse.

There are many such 'useful idiots' today, and none more so perhaps than those calling for the normalisation and promotion of gender choice for children. We are seeing, in fact, a deliberate attempt to undermine our culture, and it is dangerous. Not just to children, who are the immediate victims, but to all of us.

Most people know intuitively the extreme peril of promoting such ideas – most parents indeed feel anger at what they recognise to be the attempted exploitation and indoctrination of their children. But it is not enough just to recognise the problem. We must act now, and speak out to stem the decline.

It is time for all of us to wake up and reject this covert and insidious manipulation of the nation's young by those who seek to sow subversion and destroy society as we know it, in order to substitute and establish their own regime.

Source: Voice for Justice UK, 2022/ 23

i. We must not allow this evil to spread

Between 1941 and 1945, in what was described by the Nazis as 'the final solution to the Jewish problem', the world witnessed the systematic slaughter of over 6,000,000 Jews – men, women and children, all condemned indiscriminately to what were at the time euphemistically called 'labour camps', but in reality, were simply 'death camps.' The aim was literally to wipe out all Jews across Europe, for the simple reason that, to Hitler and his fellow Nazis, the Jewish race was subhuman and evil.

This was genocide on an unimaginable scale and in the aftermath of WW2, when the full horror of the Concentration Camps was exposed, the world vowed that such atrocities would never happen again. On 3 September 1953, The European Convention on Human Rights, designed to protect fundamental human freedoms, such as the right to life, freedom of belief, and protection from discrimination, torture, the death penalty, etc, came into force (https://www.echr.coe.int/european-convention-on-human-rights). It has remained in force for the last 70 years, as we have continued to celebrate and defend those freedoms – yet now, almost unbelievably, we are seeing that same spirit, aimed at the total annihilation of the Jews, once again manifesting on our streets.

On 7 October, the world was sickened by news of the murderous, surprise attack launched by Hamas on Israel. 1,400 died in that raid, in the main civilians simply going about their daily lives, while some 230 were kidnapped and taken back to Gaza – seemingly, as bargaining chips designed to prevent retaliation.

The attack was a declaration of war by terrorists, whose stated aim is to wipe Israel off the face of the earth (https://www.cfr.org/backgrounder/what-hamas#:~:text=In%201988%2C%20Hamas%20published%20its,Islamic%20society%20in%20historic%20Palestine).

Since that time, as Israel has sought to counter the threat of Hamas and fighting has broken out in the Gaza strip and beyond, there has been global outcry on the part of those sympathetic to the Palestinian cause for an immediate cessation to hostilities. By which it is meant, in practice, that Hamas will remain free to pursue its murderous campaign, but that Israel must not retaliate.

Let us, however, consider – from the start, Hamas have shown themselves prepared to sacrifice the Palestinian people in pursuit of their stated aim to destroy Israel. To this end, they have hidden their weapons and infrastructure amongst the civilian population, ruthlessly exploiting men, women, children, and the sick, in order to deter retaliation. Thus, rockets, used to rain down terror on Israel, have been cold-bloodedly hidden in schools and hospitals, so that if Israel dares try and eliminate them, it can be castigated for targeting civilians and breaking the rules of war.

Let us make no mistake, the goal of Islamist terror groups is not limited to Israel, but extends to the destruction of all Jewish people across the world. And, with calls for jihad and intifada ringing out from the so-called 'peace marches', those poisonous tendrils are now taking root in our own streets.

In all conscience we cannot, and must not, permit this.

It is entirely right that Israel takes appropriate and proportionate action to defend itself from threat, and those who are genuine in their calls for peace should, first and foremost, be condemning not them, but Hamas – for the good of both Jews and Palestinians alike. For genuine peace, protestors should be calling for the condemnation and removal of all terrorists from Gaza and the Palestinian territories. Because only then will the civilian population of both States be able to live in peace.

Likewise, so-called pro-Palestinian demonstrations in the UK should, in the first instance, be condemning Hamas, not Israel – castigating the terrorists for their harsh and uncaring exploitation of those who cannot defend themselves. As it is, calling for violent holy war callously disregards the ordinary citizens of Gaza and simply exposes the murderous hatred towards Israel, and indeed the West as a whole, that exists amongst some sections of society and that turns such demonstrations – as Suella Braverman has so bravely and accurately said – into hate marches, designed to foment violence and war (https://www.theguardian.com/politics/2023/oct/30/uk-ministers-cobra-meeting-terrorism-threat-israel-hamas-conflict-suella-braverman).

The suffering of the Palestinian people in Gaza is unquestionably appalling and all must want it to end. But the war, deliberately provoked and engineered by Hamas, does not and cannot justify the rise in anti-Semitism now evident of our streets, and indeed across the whole world. We are seeing the resurrection of an ancient evil, and the murderous spirit so evident in the death camps must not be allowed once again to take root in our streets. England resisted such evil in WW2, and we must resist it now.

There is compelling evidence that the campaign of protest against Israel in the UK is being manipulated by terror networks linked to Iran, shamelessly manipulating the truth in order to support their preferred narrative of Israeli oppression (https://www.thetimes.co.uk/article/iran-agents-uk-pro-palestine-protests-9f8pst6vf).

It is unquestionably this that has led to the horrifying rise in anti-Semitic attacks over the last month, with hate crimes against Jews reportedly increasing by a staggering 1,350%. The situation has indeed become so bad that many Jews in the UK are now afraid to venture out on the streets.

At every level, this is unacceptable. The authorities must act without delay to stop all demonstrations that incite hatred against the Jews, and those that advocate and endorse such behaviour must be held accountable before the law.

Source: Voice for Justice UK, 2022/ 23

j. **Order and Disorder**

There is a right order, on which the existence and wellbeing of humanity depends. And there is a 'wrong' order – a disorder – that, though it may be clothed in weasel words of reason and the best interests of all, feeds only the control of the strong. Where 'disorder' gains dominance, the rights of lesser mortals, increasingly powerless before an advancing juggernaut of oppression, are all too often overridden or crushed.

This is what we are witnessing in the casual sacrifice of the Palestinian people by those who are currently responsible for their care, namely, the terrorist group Hamas. When the terrorists launched their murderous attack on Israel on 7thOctober, they knew precisely what would happen. The desired outcome was never to uphold Palestinian freedoms, but rather to provoke war that would ignite the whole of the Middle East and spread throughout the world: to achieve their expressed aim of wiping Israel off the face of the earth. To this end, they have calculatedly and cold-bloodedly sacrificed the people they were supposed to protect, with civilian casualties and deaths ruthlessly exploited to cast Israelis – the undisputed targets of their hatred – as evil oppressors.

It is this same war that we are seeing now take root on our own streets, with cries of Jihad and Intifada echoing from the lips of those who claim to be demonstrating for peace. The Home Secretary, Suella Braverman, has rightly drawn attention to the offensive nature of some of the chants, posters and stickers that are a feature of the pro-Palestinian peace marches, and which demonstrate all too clearly the growing climate of violent anti-Semitism spreading its poison in our midst.

Despite the fact that this weekend the nation will remember and commemorate those who gave their lives that we might live, the Metropolitan Police have consistently said there are no grounds for banning potentially disruptive demonstrations that compete with that commemoration. The exclusion zone imposed round the Cenotaph late this afternoon is to be welcomed (https://www.bbc.co.uk/news/uk-67383065), but can it really be said that the police lack such power? After all, amongst other related provisions, the Public Order Act 1986 states clearly that it is an offence to stir up religious hatred (s.29B), or not to comply with a direction that may be given not to incite serious disorder, disruption of the life of the community, or intimidation. Whatever the peaceful intentions of many of the demonstrators, these elements – inciting 'hatred' against both Israel and Jews worldwide – are clearly to be anticipated, and are both disruptive and intimidating. So surely there are grounds for banning such marches this Remembrance weekend, and Suella Braverman is to be applauded for her brave stand – for daring to voice what others have lacked the courage to say.

We all want to see peace in the Middle East, but it seems that is impossible while Hamas remains in control – as, sadly, demonstrated by the events of 7th October. What is without doubt, however, is that there will be no end to conflict while there remain calls for jihad, the death of all Jews, and intifada (violent uprising) 'from London to Jerusalem'.

It is no surprise that Jews living in Britain are becoming increasingly fearful, and all such incitement must be resisted. We must not let violence take root on our streets – we're better than that! But people need leadership, and the truth is we need more politicians who will not be afraid to confront hatred and bigotry, whenever and wherever it rears its ugly head.

Source: Voice for Justice UK, 2022/ 23

k. Debunking the copyright excuse – A welcome encouragement for parents

In a welcome but long overdue move, Education Secretary Gillian Keegan (October 2023) has now written to schools telling them to share with parents, on request, all materials scheduled for use in relationships, sex and health education (RSHE). Parents, she says, have the right to know what children are taught, and schools can no longer be permitted to block access because of supposed copyright issues (https://www.dailymail.co.uk/news/article-12663819/Schools-sex-education-material-Education-Parent-asks-Secretary-Gillian-Keegan-warns.html).

She went on to state that copyright obligations relating to sex education materials are trumped in law by the parent's right to know, and the Department for Education is now reportedly preparing template letters to counter possible claims by providers for copyright infringement.

Well and good and, as said, the statement is extremely welcome. There remain, however, a few very large elephants in the room – chief of which, is how we got into this position in the first place. Parents, after all, entrust their child to a school to be 'educated', so that they might best realise their potential and be prepared to take their future place in society. In this regard, the school should act under the direction of a child's parents and does not, of itself, have any right to dictate what a child learns. While a child remains on school premises, the school is literally *in loco parentis;* which means that it is under a duty to act subject to the parents' directions and has no right to exceed that mandate.

What it must not do is indoctrinate children into acceptance and practice of questionable and hazardous behaviours for the purpose of bringing about wider social change.

Protocol 1, Article 2 of the Human Rights Act 1998 states, 'In the exercise of any functions which it assumes in relation to education and to teaching, the State shall respect the right of parents to ensure such education and teaching is in conformity with their own religious and philosophical onvictions'(https://www.equality humanrights.com/en/human-rights-act/article-2-first-protocol-right-education).

Patently, this is something many schools are failing to do, often to the extent of deliberately ignoring or even over-riding the protests of parents who oppose the promotion of sexual licence, same sex behaviours, and gender choice – not just on religious grounds, but because they think such teaching puts their children at risk.

Schools claim that they are acting solely for the benefit of children, protecting them against exploitation and abuse in an increasingly dangerous world ... and that, where there are objections, they know better than parents. But the question must surely be asked, if the disputed resources are as good as claimed and beneficial, why do so many schools actively try and stop parents from seeing them?

The unpalatable answer would seem to be that in recent years schools have not just knowingly and recklessly exceeded their brief, but have become proactive agents for ideological change, teaching highly disputed and potentially damaging concepts as incontrovertible 'fact'. It could even perhaps be said that, if secular activists advocating sexual libertarianism have acted as architects for cultural revolution, then schools have become one of the main agents for its implementation. Uncoupling the stranglehold of these ideologues is undeniably now going to present a challenge, but, for the sake of the nation's young, it is a challenge that must be faced. The harmful indoctrination of children must end.

Later this year, the Government is set to launch a consultation into how to ensure 'that all RSHE teaching is factual and does not present contested views on sensitive topics as fact' (https://questions-statements.parliament.uk/written-statements/detail/2023-06-05/hcws814). The aim, it further says, is to put it place "clear safeguards to stop pupils from being taught contested and potentially damaging concepts". This too is to be welcomed.

But not only must parents be given the automatic right to see all materials to which their children will be exposed – the ideologues with their pernicious agenda for change must now be removed.

Source: Voice for Justice UK, 2022/ 23

3. POLITICAL – HEALTH SERVICE

a. No to Euthanasia! - The legalisation of assisted suicide must be resisted

On 15th June 2023, the Royal College of Surgeons (RCS) announced that it would no longer oppose assisted dying, but would officially adopt a neutral stance, bringing it into line with the British Medical Association, the Royal College of Physicians and the Royal College of Nursing, all of which bodies in the last few years have, by implication, aligned themselves with activist groups calling for what they inappropriately label 'reform'.

In a Press release euphorically issued by Dignity in Dying (Royal College of Surgeons drops opposition to assisted dying as survey finds majority of members support law change - Dignity in Dying), Professor Sir John Graham-Temple, former president of the RCS, is quoted as saying, 'While the views of the medical profession are an important part of this debate, doctors should not dictate to society the choices that people are able to make about their own lives and deaths. We must listen to and respect the wishes of those we treat …'

This general statement is fine so far as it goes, especially if coupled with adherence to the law, but this is something that the medical profession at the moment is signally failing to do. As highlighted in a recent report by the Lords and Commons Family and Child Protection Group, ***When End of Life Care Goes Wrong***, too many of the elderly and vulnerable who are admitted to hospital – sometimes for relatively trivial complaints, such as constipation – find themselves inappropriately and prematurely placed on an end of life care plan. Though in theory designed to give a patient the best end of life care that they and their family would choose, in practice assessment all too often becomes a tick box exercise, leading to the prescription of treatment all too often imposed without the patient's agreement or even knowledge, and designed to bring about death.

But there is more. Many patients aged 60+ routinely have a Do Not Resuscitate (DNR) order attached to their notes – on the flimsiest of grounds that should, God forbid, something happen (such as a heart attack), they would not wish to endure the pain and discomfort of resuscitation. Sounds perhaps reasonable, but what many of the public don't know is that DNR orders, once triggered, are accompanied by a cessation of medication and the total withdrawal of food and hydration. Which can hold good, even when the patient is begging for a drink. At the same time, drugs such as midazolam and morphine – both useful drugs, correctly prescribed – are inappropriately and unnecessarily administered, with the sole aim of rendering the patient comatose, and hastening death.

In other words, and to put it bluntly, a frightening number of patients being admitted to hospital are already being subjected

to managed death, despite the fact such treatment is currently prohibited under UK law and is liable to criminal prosecution.

All of us, I imagine, hope for a 'good' death, with minimal pain and our loved ones gathered round to say goodbye. Campaigners for assisted suicide would add that those suffering from terminal illness, in what they claim is unbearable pain, must have the right to choose for themselves the time and manner of their death, further arguing that they have the support of 84% of the British public, similarly calling for change.

But, if the figure quoted is accurate, how far can it be trusted? How much do the British public really understand what's at stake?

In recent years there has been unremitting pressure in the media to legalise assisted dying, and it's without question that you would have to have a heart of stone to force someone to endure unnecessary pain. But the arguments put forward by euthanasia campaigners distort what for many is the reality of approaching death. Palliative care in the UK is amongst the best in the world, and it is expressly designed to minimise suffering. But infinitely worse is the wilful and shocking disregard of evidenced coercion of those who actually want to live, and who are being denied the right to die 'naturally', in accordance with their wishes.

If assisted suicide for those judged to be in the last months of life should become legal, we already know from the evidence of places such as Canada (https://apnews.com/article/covid-science-health-toronto-7c631558a457188d2bd2b5cfd360a867), Belgium, and the Netherlands that it will be but a short step from there to the mandated killing of the mentally ill and depressed – those in fact who simply feel they can no longer go on. And on current evidence, even children will become subject to this legalised culling (https://www.theguardian.com/society/2023/apr/14/netherlands-to-broaden-euthanasia-rules-to-cover-children-of-all-ages). Is this really what we want to endorse as a society – the tidying away of those not actively contributing to what we perceive as the general good? The removal of those draining our resources?

Sounds unbelievable perhaps, but, as sure as night follows day, this will happen, because as we're seeing in reports from Canada and the US, with medical costs for treatment now so high, insurers are already refusing to fund medication and offering instead to provide medical assistance in dying (https://www.dailymail.co.uk/news/article-11135637/Canadian-veteran-offered-EUTHANASIA-called-Veteran-Affairs-Canada-hotline-help.html).

With many hospitals in the UK already making value judgments as to whether or not someone's life is worth preserving, where would the proposed reforms, being endorsed by implication by the RCS, leave us? At the very least such a position is a betrayal of the Hippocratic oath – not actually sworn by doctors today, of course, but handed down from antiquity – to prescribe only beneficial treatments and to refrain from causing harm or hurt. But infinitely worse, such an approach denies the respect, dignity and care towards others mandated by God.

Since the publication of the LCFCPG Report *When End of Life Care Goes Wrong*, the number of complaints from those whose loved ones have prematurely and inappropriately died following admission to hospital, has literally sky rocketed. Coming up to around 900 at the last count, and rising daily – the tip of a very large iceberg. It is no exaggeration to say that people in this country are becoming terrified of going into hospital.

So, given the display of such horrifying inhumanity towards those who cannot defend themselves, the question must be asked – what are the Royal Colleges really saying, when they state they are going to adopt a neutral position towards 'assisted' death? Do they really mean people must be allowed to choose for themselves whether they live or die – or do they rather mean that, in these days of over-stretched resources, they will sanction the legalised killing of those regarded as not contributing to the general good?

Source: Voice for Justice UK, 2022/ 23

b. 10 million aborted – 10 million arrived

"Foreigners who live in your land will gain more power"
Deuteronomy 28:43 (NKJV)

According to latest figures from the UK's Office for National Statistics (ONS), between the years 2011-2021, the number of foreign born people in England and Wales grew from 7.5 million to 16.8 million, with the greatest number of migrants coming from India, Poland, and Pakistan, in that order.

In a report on the figures, The Times headed its article, *Ten million residents of England and Wales born outside the UK, 2021 census shows* (https://www.thetimes.co.uk/article/ten-million-residents-of-england-and-wales-born-outside-the-uk-2021-census-shows-jzh7pmplm).

Now this is interesting, not so much for what it tells us about immigration, but for the fact the number of migrants precisely matches the number of babies that have been aborted in England and Wales since 1967.

Coincidence? Or is the number of lives lost being replaced by some sort of cosmic process of redress? To put it another way, because of the wanton and sinful sacrifice of our unborn, is our 'country' now being given over to others?

To those without faith, the notion may appear absurd, but consider – at every level we are seeing today an unremitting erosion of what up to now has been our culture, tradition, and values. Now it may be argued that the changes, and those who have brought them about, are a bit like the proverbial curates' egg – a mix of good and bad – but whatever your view, it is without doubt that the face of the country is changing, and that there is a growing climate of instability. The news at the moment, for example, is dominated by the escalating crisis of how we should respond to illegal immigration and, on any assessment, we appear to be sliding ever deeper into chaos, with no easy solution in view.

Those of us with faith say it is clear that, because of our sinful contempt for God, combined with our behaviour and wanton destruction of life, He has withdrawn His protection. But can it be that these figures suggest something more? Can it be that, as result of our choices, God has not just withdrawn His shield, but is now *actively* giving us over to the consequences of what the Bible clearly labels sin?

Is it, in fact, payback time?

We would perhaps do well to consider the curses spelt out for disobedience to the laws laid down by God – for our own protection and wellbeing – in Deuteronomy, in particular **Deuteronomy 28:43-45 (NKJV):** *"⁴³ "The alien who is among you shall rise higher and higher above you, and you shall come down lower and lower. ⁴⁴ He shall lend to you, but you shall not lend to him; he shall be the head, and you shall be the tail.*
⁴⁵ "Moreover all these curses shall come upon you and pursue and overtake you, until you are destroyed, because you did not obey the voice of the Lord your God, to keep His commandments and His statutes which He commanded you."
Let us make no mistake, God could solve the UK's many problems in a heartbeat, but while we persist in our hubris, rejecting all idea of obedience, He will not intervene. For our nation to survive, it is both urgent and vital that we reacquaint ourselves with God's word and repent. Before it is too late.

Source: Voice for Justice UK, 2022/ 23

c. **RSHE – STI figures published**

Children's Commissioner Dame Rachel de Souza is reported as saying that a fear of teaching sex education in schools is driving a rise in sexually transmitted diseases (https://www.telegraph.co.uk/news/2023/11/10/schools-fear-teaching-sex-education-driving-rise-in-sti/). As a remedy for this, she is calling for increased and better sex education, that will keep children safe.

At one level, she is of course entirely right. In the sexually exploitative and abusive climate that has become the norm, children need to be educated to ensure their best protection. But this begs the question, how precisely is that to be achieved?

Facts: According to the UK Health Security Agency, which provides data on STI diagnoses and sexual health services, recorded STI infections for 2022 show that, with 82,592 identified cases of gonorrhoea, diagnoses are now at their highest level since records began in 1918. With regards young people specifically, the figures show that in 2022, 10,053 cases of gonorrhoea were diagnosed among children aged between 13 to 19 years old. Chlamydia diagnoses also increased by 24.3%, from 160,279 in 2021 to 199,233 in 2022, while infectious syphilis diagnoses went up 15% for the same period. Taken together, this means that, although STI diagnoses are increasing overall across the nation, by far the highest increase in infection has been amongst young people aged 15-24, closely followed by gay, bisexual, and other men who have sex with men (https://www.gov.uk/government/statistics/sexually-transmitted-infections-stis-annual-data-tables/sexually-transmitted-infections-and-screening-for-chlamydia-in-england-2022-report).

If we look a little further back to 2002, the total number of diagnoses of gonorrhoea for young people aged 16-19 was 6,806, while there were 47 recorded cases for syphilis – which figures, it was said, showed a massive increase on numbers recorded in the 1990s. The 2004 Parliamentary report, Teenage Sexual Health (https://www.parliament.uk/globalassets/documents/post/postpn2 17.pdf) attributes the increase to a lowering of the age for first intercourse; a higher acquisition rate for new partners than for other age groups; and an increased likelihood of being involved in two or more sexual relationships simultaneously.

The questions must surely, therefore, be asked (1) where and how have children over the past three decades 'learnt' these behaviours and (2) how have they been persuaded to adopt and indulge such morally lax practices, that all too clearly expose them to harm?

On any scale, the latest figures are alarming, and we clearly do need to do something to address the problem - hopefully reversing the trend. Dame Rachel de Souza has recommended increasing what she calls 'better' sex education, with safeguarding made a priority. But we should perhaps unpack exactly what it is she is advocating here, because what she clearly says, as reported in The Times article of 10 November (https://www.thetimes.co.uk/article/sex-education-culture-wars-driving-shocking-increase-in-std-s-among-children-times-health-commission-b7ds9zsmx) is that children should be provided with more detailed teaching on the basics of sex, so as to counter misleading and damaging pornographic material to which they all have access on the internet, and which is currently influencing their behaviour.

Clearly, more does need to be done to keep children safe online, but will giving children more detailed information on the mechanics of sex in class really help the problem, or will it simply make matters worse? After all, over the past couple of decades, mandated sex education – deliberately stripped of any kind of moral frame, so that children don't feel 'judged' – has without doubt, and sometimes overtly, encouraged experimentation and promiscuity. You can't know 'what you are, or what you like' the argument runs, until you've tried it for yourself – so children have been encouraged to experiment with different kinds of relationships, as well as different behaviours, despite the fact some of those behaviours – such as anal intercourse, and fisting – are hazardous and will put them at risk of harm.

Yes, children need to be armed against sexual exploitation and abuse, but this should be by alerting them to the dangers of premature sexual activity and promiscuity. They should be taught that they are special, and that sex is a precious gift, not to be lightly given away. Both boys and girls need to be taught that sex is not simply a 'consensual' leisure activity, on a par with hooking up for coffee. And, girls especially need to be taught not just that they have an absolute right to say no, free of peer expectation or pressure, but that their future wellbeing and happiness will be best served by not indulging in casual and/or unusual sex. And both sexes need to be taught that a baby is precious, and a gift – not simply an inconvenience to be disposed of, if unwanted.

It has long been argued that RSE teaching contains inappropriate materials, that, far from keeping children safe, promote premature and medically hazardous sexual behaviour. The latest figures for STI rates should justifiably cause alarm, but to reduce them we need to attack the problem at source – which means that we must urgently address why young people have become so lax in their approach to sex. Unfashionable though it may seem, we need once again to teach children the values of purity, commitment, responsibility, and fidelity. We need, in a nutshell, to teach them to say 'No'.

Source: Voice for Justice UK, 2022/ 23

d. When ideology becomes 'fact'

Three extremely interesting articles all appeared on the same day this week. First, as part of a new NHS sexual orientation and gender identity form, the Telegraph reported that in some hospitals, doctors are now being asked to detail their patient's sexual orientation, gender, sex assigned at birth, preferred pronouns, whether or not they have transitioned, and any known future plans to change gender. They are also required to record what 'organs' the patient currently has, namely, do they have a penis or a vagina, and were these organs present at birth, or have they been surgically enhanced or constructed (https://www.telegraph.co.uk/news/2023/11/27/doctors-have-to-tick-whether-patient-has-a-penis-or-vagina/). This information, so far being gathered at King's College Hospital, Guy's and St Thomas' Hospital, the Frimley Health NHS Trust, and the Maudsley Trust, is set be adopted as part of an electronic patient record system throughout the NHS. It has no obvious connection or bearing on the condition for which patients are admitted.

Second, it was reported that the eagerly anticipated, but long overdue, transgender guidance for schools is at long last to be published and that, while children will be allowed to socially transition with the consent of their parents, teachers will not be compelled to address such children by their 'chosen pronoun' (https://www.thetimes.co.uk/article/trans-gender-guidance-schools-uk-published-7cnc0f596). School lavatories and changing rooms will also be kept separate, and contact sports will remain separated by biological sex. In a seeming policy volte face, one government source has also reportedly said that there will be a presumption *against* encouraging social transitioning, though an all-out plan to ban children from changing their gender identity below the age of 18 has been dropped.

This particular report is a significant victory for parents, long worried by the harms to which their children are being exposed as result of the ideological normalisation and promotion of gender choice. It is disappointing, however, in that it still leaves open the door for children below the age of 18 to make life-changing decisions that they may, in time, bitterly regret.

Third, it appears that as result of complaints by a number of charities, led by the LGBTQ+ campaigning group Stonewall, the UK's Equality and Human Rights Commission (EHRC) might now be blacklisted by the UN Human Rights Council because of its position on biological sex (https://www.telegraph.co.uk/news/2023/11/27/britain-faces-un-blacklist-over-trans-rights-lobby-ehrc/#:~:text=The%20UK%27s%20Equalities%20and%20Human,Stonewall%2C%20the%20controversial%20LGBT%20charity). If the complaints are upheld, this will downgrade the UK from A to B status, thus effectively barring us from taking part in any UN discussions and policy decisions on human rights, and putting us on a par with countries such as Qatar, Zimbabwe, and the Democratic Republic of Congo.

What has provoked such ire on the part of trans campaigning groups?

The answer is not hard to find. Stonewall is apparently objecting to advice given by the EHRC that the term 'sex' should be redefined under law as 'biological sex'. The stated reasoning of the EHRC is that this would provide greater clarity for the determination of contentious issues, such as the use of single sex spaces. But, to Stonewall, the very idea that women should be entitled to access and quiet enjoyment of their own 'space' is manifestation of despicable bigotry. Never mind the rising number of sexual assault and rape cases as result of unrestricted access to such areas, or the need for privacy, anyone who supports such views must be taken down! Stonewall's distorted version of 'reality' must prevail.

If proof were needed of the ideological battle currently raging to reconfigure society, it is surely provided by these three articles. In our brave new world, where Self reigns supreme, 'truth' is being cast as subjective. I am whatever I say I am, and if your 'truth' disputes that, then, whatever it takes, you must be silenced. No mercy!

Let us not be deceived. At heart, this is manifestation of the age-old battle between the devil and God, with Satan denying reality and fighting to assert control. Persuading men and women to deny the truth of their being is at heart demonic temptation, second only to the enticement to destroy one's own life, flinging back the gift in the face of the Creator.

The imposition of such a distorted view of reality must be resisted – not because we are hate-filled bigots, denying others the right to be fully themselves, but because true happiness and peace can only be found in embracing and becoming fully what God has made and intends us to be. And that means recognising the reality of biological sex.

Source: Voice for Justice UK, 2022/ 23

4. POLITICAL – THE ENVIROMENT

a. The World's Population

It is estimated that since the Year 5000Bc, the world population was approx. five million. It has been acknowledged that up to 1804 the world's global population was one billion, and within 120 years doubled to two billion by 1927.

Since then and particularly the past fifty years, the global population has increased from 3.7 billion in 1971 to circ. 8 billion (2023), as illustrated in **Table 1**.

The increased rate of the global population since 1927 clearly dispels the theory of evolution (and Darwinism) as a lie. Any notion of population growth via evolution (to current numbers - eight billion), would have happened millions of years ago, causing worldwide famine and starvation; to which we wouldn't existed now!

In fact if evolution did occur, then the question is who controlled and maintained the level of population growth which we have today??

What does the Bible say about population control / depopulation?

The Bible doesn't say anything about population control. Instead, humans are told to "be fruitful and multiply" (**Genesis 1:22, 28**). **Psalm 127:3–5** tells us that children are a heritage from the Lord and that the fruit of the womb is a reward from Him.

Genesis 1:22 (NKJV)
²² And God blessed them, saying, "Be fruitful and multiply, and fill the waters in the seas, and let birds multiply on the earth."

Genesis 1:28 (NKJV)
²⁸ Then God blessed them, and God said to them, "Be fruitful and multiply; fill the earth and subdue it; have dominion over the fish of the sea, over the birds of the air, and over every living thing that moves on the earth."

Psalm 127:3-5 (NKJV)
³ Behold, children are a heritage from the Lord,
The fruit of the womb is a reward.
⁴ Like arrows in the hand of a warrior,
So are the children of one's youth.
⁵ Happy is the man who has his quiver full of them;
They shall not be ashamed,
But shall speak with their enemies in the gate.

At the time of this writing, there are approximately 8 billion people in the world. That's a lot of people, but to put that number in perspective, there are about 7.5 trillion square feet of land in the state of Texas, in the United States, alone. This means that, theoretically, every person in the world could fit in the state of Texas, and each person would have 1,056 square feet of living space—4,224 square feet for a family of four! One might say that the problem is not the number of people but rather the lack of resources (food, water, etc.) and the ability to distribute those resources.

If all the people on Earth could fit comfortably in Texas, imagine all the room people would have if they spread out evenly over an entire continent. How much room would everyone have if all of Africa (11.7 million square miles), for example, was used for housing? (The answer is about 1 acre per person.) Even if we remove the Sahara Desert from the equation, Africa, the second-largest continent, would have plenty of living space for every person on the planet and still have room for water, arable land, and roads and other infrastructure. The point is, the earth has lots of room, and the world's population should not need to be "controlled."

Of course, there are certain areas of the world that are overpopulated—that is to say, certain metropolitan areas contain an unhealthy *concentration* of a region's population. People continue to migrate in large numbers into urban centres that are ill-equipped to handle the influx. The poverty, disease, and crime that overcrowding engenders are tragic to behold. There are no easy answers to the problem of urban overcrowding, but there is nothing wrong with programs to build more housing, increase the labour force, and provide education and birth control.

Unfortunately, those who advocate population control often support ungodly methods of control, such as abortion, euthanasia, and forced sterilization. Schemes such as forced abortion directly conflict with the Bible's teaching that human life is sacred. Many promoters of population control advance policies that presuppose the problem is too many humans, while the real problem is ignored.

The root problem is neither population size nor resource availability. The problem is sin. Selfish, sinful, and power-hungry people have misused God's creation. God intended that man have dominion over the rest of creation (**Genesis 1:26**). Men were to be stewards of the earth, and **1 Corinthians 4:2** adds that "it is required of stewards that they be found trustworthy" (NKJV). Sadly, corrupt governments, rather than acting as trustworthy stewards of a country's resources, often hoard food, mismanage resources, and squander money instead of seeing that their own people are fed. Unscrupulous corporations, too, strive for more control of the food supply and seem more willing to strike lucrative deals than to benefit society.

Genesis 1:26 (NKJV)
²⁶ Then God said, "Let Us make man in Our image, according to Our likeness; let them have dominion over the fish of the sea, over the birds of the air, and over the cattle, over all the earth and over every creeping thing that creeps on the earth."

1 Corinthians 4:2 (NKJV)
² Moreover it is required in stewards that one be found faithful.

The biblical answer to "overpopulation" is not to demand fewer people, especially if that involves culling the current population. The biblical answer is to honour people enough to provide for their needs (see **Mark 12:31**). There may be a problem with how the population is distributed and with how resources are managed, but the problem is not too many people on Earth. Greed, lust for power, and foolishness lead to the mishandling of resources, and millions of people suffer as a result.

Mark 12:31 (NKJV)

³¹ And the second, like it, is this: 'You shall love your neighbour as yourself.' There is no other commandment greater than these."

Table 1 – World Population

Year	World Population	Year	World Population	Year	World Population
-5000	5,000,000	1500	450,000,000	1959	2,970,292,188
-4000	7,000,000	1600	500,000,000	1960	3,019,233,434
-3000	14,000,000	1700	610,000,000	1961	3,068,370,609
-2000	27,000,000	1760	770,000,000	1962	3,126,686,743
-1000	50,000,000	1804	1,000,000,000	1963	3,195,779,247
-500	100,000,000	1850	1,200,000,000	1964	3,267,212,338
-200	150,000,000	1900	1,600,000,000	1965	3,337,111,983
200	190,000,000	1927	2,000,000,000	1966	3,406,417,036
600	200,000,000	1951	2,543,130,380	1967	3,475,448,166
700	210,000,000	1952	2,590,270,899	1968	3,546,810,808
800	220,000,000	1953	2,640,278,797	1969	3,620,655,275
900	240,000,000	1954	2,691,979,339	1970	3,695,390,336
1000	275,000,000	1955	2,746,072,141	1971	3,770,163,092
1100	320,000,000	1956	2,801,002,631	1972	3,844,800,885
1400	350,000,000	1957	2,857,866,857	1973	3,920,251,504
1200	360,000,000	1958	2,916,108,097	1974	3,995,517,077

Year	World Population	Year	World Population	Year	World Population
1975	4,069,437,231	1992	5,492,686,093	2008	6,811,597,272
1976	4,142,505,882	1993	5,577,433,523	2009	6,898,305,908
1977	4,215,772,490	1994	5,660,727,993	2010	6,985,603,105
1978	4,289,657,708	1995	5,743,219,454	2011	7,073,125,425
1979	4,365,582,871	1996	5,825,145,298	2012	7,161,697,921
1980	4,444,007,706	1997	5,906,481,261	2013	7,250,593,370
1981	4,524,627,658	1998	5,987,312,480	2014	7,339,013,419
1982	4,607,984,871	1999	6,067,758,458	2015	7,426,597,537
1983	4,691,884,238	2000	6,148,898,975	2016	7,513,474,238
1984	4,775,836,074	2001	6,230,746,982	2017	7,599,822,404
1985	4,861,730,613	2002	6,312,407,360	2018	7,683,789,828
1986	4,950,063,339	2003	6,393,898,365	2019	7,764,951,032
1987	5,040,984,495	2004	6,475,751,478	2020	7,840,952,880
1988	5,132,293,974	2005	6,558,176,119	2021	7,909,295,151
1989	5,223,704,308	2006	6,641,416,218	2022	7,975,105,156
1990	5,316,175,862	2007	6,725,948,544	2023	8,045,311,447
1991	5,406,245,867				

Source: https://www.worldmeters.info

b. Global Boiling

This was the warning of United Nations Secretary-General Antonio Guterres, in a speech made in response to a report by scientists from the European Copernicus Climate Change Service and World Meteorological Organisation, stating that July 2023 was set to be the world's hottest month on record (https://www.theguardian.com/science/2023/jul/27/scientists-july-world-hottest-month-record-climate-temperatures).

Meanwhile, in his one-man campaign to save the planet, London Mayor Sadiq Khan has won the right to roll out his controversial Ultra Low Emission Zone (Ulez) across the whole of London (https://www.thetimes.co.uk/article/ulez-expansion-london-high-court-ruling-2023-sadiq-khan-8h65kk8qx).

What *on earth* is going on? Is Secretary-General Guterres right, and we're all doomed unless we cut out all carbon, gas, foreign holidays, and meat? And is Sadiq Khan the brave forerunner of humanity's salvation? If we stop within our 15 minute zones (https://www.euronews.com/green/2023/02/21/what-is-a-15-minute-city-the-eco-concept-that-has-been-jumped-on-by-conspiracy-theorists), can we even now reverse this horrific trend?

Climate activists would have us believe we can. The problems we face, they say heatedly, are purely the result of mankind's selfish exploitation of planet earth. So, just as we have caused the problems, now we can put them right. So fervently do they believe this, that to all intents and purposes 'climate' has become a new religion.

Friends of the Earth, Extinction Rebellion, Climate Action ... Stop Oil, and many more, are brave acolytes of this new faith, and they will seemingly stop at nothing to proselytise the unredeemed and save humanity. As for any part God may have to play ... such an idea would seem to be a bit of a non-starter. For our eco warriors, God – if He exists at all, which most of them appear to doubt – either doesn't care or, more to the point, is powerless. They are absolute in the conviction that it's down to us to become the architects of our own salvation.

Well and good. Certainly, we should do all we can to protect our world. But it is well said that the proof of the pudding is in the eating, and the obvious question is, can they deliver? On current evidence, the answer to that would seem to be a resounding no. If anything, in fact, the downward spiral of planet earth into chaos would seem to be increasing. So is it not perhaps time for them, and all of us, to consider Plan B?

The Bible teaches that God is the Creator and Sovereign of all, and that He intimately cares for the whole of His creation. He is a God who not just sees, but who responds. In particular, God responds to evil and to our failure to observe His commands. Not because He's nasty and vicious and wants us to live in servitude to a list of unreasonable decrees – but because those commands, as set down in the Bible, are the template for our existence. If followed, they set us 'free', leading to peace, harmony, fulfilment and joy. If ignored, they operate to our destruction.

Across the world, over the last hundred or so years, men and women have increasingly denied God, prioritising their own selfish and self-centred 'wants' over anything and everything else. We have made gods of self-gratification, consumerism, and sexual licence – in our hubris, even attempting to rewrite creation. The result has been a progressive breakdown in social order, with ever-increasing violence on our streets, and even in our homes, and horrifying rates of mental illness, anxiety, and depression that seem to affect both young and old alike. Our sacrifice on the altar of self-indulgence and excess has yielded only bitterness, enslavement, and death.

So yes, our own actions have brought about climate change – but not in the way climate change campaigners would have us believe. If we simply follow their demands now, we will only fall deeper into the pit, becoming victim to the strangulation of an authoritarian ideology that will not allow dissent. In fact, the *only* way we can save ourselves from the suffocating and suppurating chaos that seems increasingly to dominate the world, is by repenting our rebellion against God, and turning back to Him before it all becomes too late.

The Bible promises that if we will only humble ourselves and pray, turning from our wicked ways, then God will hear us from heaven and forgive … and will heal the land (**2 Chronicles 7:14, NKJV**).

God commanded us, at our creation, to care for the Earth. That is still His command to us today. If we turn to Him and repent, then God – Creator of the Sun, Moon, stars, and Earth, and Lord of the wind and rain – will help. Yes, we are obliged to do what we can, but to succeed, we must act only in obedience to God and with His guidance.

But should we remain obdurate and refuse His Lordship and guidance, then no amount of effort, however well-intentioned, can save us from the judgement that even now hammers at the door.

Source: Voice for Justice UK, 2022/ 23

c. What's God's take on climate change? (As greenhouses gases continue to soar, what might God be saying?)

Salvation apparently looms, if we will all only do 'our bit'! So claim climate change activists and extinction rebels, who, when they're not gluing themselves to busy roads and orchestrating mass campaigns for non-violent civil disobedience, are agitating for a global cut to carbon emissions and improved home insulation, which, they say, is the only way to save planet earth.

The UN global climate change conference in 2021, COP26 in Glasgow, was a response to growing fears of global destruction if the rise in temperature is not brought under control. It is being hailed as a last chance for countries to band together to try and agree measures that will turn back the tide before it all becomes too late – which time, if Sir David Attenborough is to be believed, was actually round about yesterday (https://www.bbc.co.uk/news/science-environment-59039485)!

Nevertheless, scientists say that there remains a narrow but rapidly closing window, so COP26 is, amongst other things, aimed at getting agreement for achieving carbon net zero emissions by 2050. To paraphrase the words of Alok Sharma, COP President-Designate (https://ukcop26.org/wp-content/uploads/2021/07/ COP

26-Explained.pdf), this is our chance not just to save the planet, but to build back better and greener!

How realistic is this? Despite the much-hyped aspirations, Prime Minister Boris Johnson, who is hosting the summit, is reportedly less than sanguine over its prospects for success, saying that it is 'touch and go' whether key goals will be met (https://www.standard.co.uk/news/uk/boris-johnson-prime-minister-glasgow-downing-street-australia-b962342.html). And given the track record for co-operation and collaboration that exists between nations, one suspects he may well be right.

China, after all, is already proving reluctant to commit itself, while President Xi refused to attend due to Covid (https://news.sky.com/story/china-details-carbon-emissions-plans-but-offers-no-new-pledges-ahead-of-cop26-12443988).

Similarly, Russian President Vladimir Putin and Brazilian President Jair Bolsonaro have also both declined. And while US President Joe Biden did put in an appearance, there are question marks over American commitment to carbon reduction policy.

So does this mean that planet Earth is now doomed, with temperatures set to rise beyond those which can support life; with rising sea levels swallowing up vast chunks of habitable land; and with extreme weather conditions, bringing in their wake apocalyptic devastation?

The answer you give to this will depend on where you sit in the debate. Climate change activists scream planetary doom, unless we take immediate action – science, properly applied, they say, can fix it all. We must fly less, give up meat, and live more sustainably! But, on the other side, those who remain unconvinced point to the normal climatic fluctuations already experienced over the lifetime of our planet, producing at various times both extreme heat and extreme cold. Indeed, all things considered, there seems strong evidence to support this view. And yet ... and yet the scale and speed of change does appear extraordinary, and it does raise concern.

So, what is God saying to the world in all of this?

It is believed by Christians that humanity is being given a warning. The reality would appear to suggest that nothing we can do will reverse the disaster looming over us, as even the UN admits (https://www.bbc.co.uk/news/science-environment-59049770). If we are lucky, and by some miracle COP26 succeeds in forging agreement for zero net carbon emissions by 2050, that doesn't resolve the problem of how we then compensate for the carbon being released into the atmosphere as a result of the melting of the permafrost, conservatively estimated as containing four times the combined amount of CO_2 emitted by modern humans (https://www.nature.com/articles/d41586-021-00659-y).

Yes, the world is at a tipping point. But while we try and combat rising temperatures and extreme weather by our own puny efforts, we don't stand a chance; nature will always be one step ahead. To have any chance of winning this battle, therefore, we need the help of the One who called all of life into being, and who alone has control over nature.

For too long humanity has treated God with contempt. We can do whatever we want, we've said. We can live as we want, have what we want ... behave as we want. We don't need a kill-joy fairy in the sky and His outdated morality! We're all 'god' now. So, in our hubris, we've rebranded good as evil, and evil as good.

But to echo the words of St Paul, *'God is not mocked ... whatsoever a man soweth, that shall he also reap'* (**Galatians 6:7**).

The climate is only part of the world that God created and of which He made us stewards. If we wish creation, including ourselves, to remain healthy and flourish, we must strive to obey God's will for the whole. We can't pick and choose. We can't ask Him to 'fulfil' our desires ... unless we obey His will. And if we are alerted to something going wrong in one part of creation, then we must ask whether it signifies that there are other things we must put right in order to restore balance.

We cannot ignore God's commands and reject the values on which life is founded, without consequence. *We do not have the right* to determine who may or may not be born, merely to allow satisfaction of our desire for sex without commitment. *We do not have the right* to play God, deciding at the end of life when a person is no longer of value and should be terminated. *We do not have the right* to redefine God's gift of marriage and question our creation as men and women, together and jointly made in His image.

In recent world events – including climate change, Covid-19, and disruption of the global economy – we are surely reaping the whirlwind. Yet God, because of His love, is giving us a chance to repent. Before it all becomes too late. The question is, are we listening? Will we hear?

Source: Voice for Justice UK, 2022/ 23

5. THE MONARCHY (THE CHURCH OF ENGLAND AND POLITICAL SYSTEM)

a. Defender of the Faith or defender of faith?

In a reception at Buckingham Palace on 23 September 2022, King Charles assured assembled faith leaders from various religions that he would work to protect the space for faith (https://www.dailymail.co.uk/news/article-11220769/King-Charles-tells-religious-leaders-Buckingham-Palace-protect-space-faith.html).

Waxing lyrical, he continued that it was his duty "to protect the diversity of our country, including by protecting the space for faith itself and its practice through the religions, cultures, traditions and beliefs to which our hearts and minds direct us as individuals." He went on to say that, as a member of the Church of England, his personal beliefs had love at their very heart, so that he was committed to respect those who follow other spiritual paths, as well as those who seek to live their lives in accordance with secular ideals.

Interesting. At her coronation in 1953, Queen Elizabeth, as head of the Anglican Church, swore to do her utmost to maintain the laws of God and the true profession of the Gospel, doing all in her power to maintain in the United Kingdom the Protestant Reformed Religion. She further swore to maintain and preserve the settlement of the Church of England, and its doctrine, worship, discipline and government, as established by English law (https://www.royal.uk/coronation-oath-2-june-1953).

This oath, taken by the sovereign, was laid down by statute in 1688. Since that time there have been occasional attempts to amend it, but the legality of such amendments remains questionable (https://www.cambridge.org/core/journals/ecclesiastical-law-journal/article/coronation-oath/F83079759125218B8D97BA1722954CBC). Are we to infer, however, that Charles is now proposing a radical rewording of the Oath that will fundamentally undermine our constitution?

Our new King is undeniably well-meaning and, according to his lights, attempting to continue the tradition of faithful service to the nation so well exemplified by his mother. We both applaud and support him in his commitment. But, in this area at least, his approach appears to be misconceived. The UK remains essentially a Christian country. Our laws and culture are founded on Christian values and belief – which values have rightly made us the envy of the world. In the national interest, they must be upheld.

Today our society is undeniably diverse, playing host to a variety of different beliefs and cultures, some of which sit uneasily alongside each other. Witness, for example, the current violent unrest between Hindus and Muslims in Leicester, that erupted following a cricket match (https://www.bbc.co.uk/news/uk-england-leicestershire-62946146). Given our now ethnically diverse population, such cultural conflict is perhaps a reality that, in the years to come, we may well see increase, and that will undoubtedly pose something of a challenge if we are to maintain peace, while helping people live in genuine tolerance and harmony. But saying that *all* beliefs are of equal value is not the answer.

Yes, as Christians we need to respect and love others – but that does not mean that we should unquestioningly accept their beliefs as of equal validity to those which, for around 1,500 years, have provided the foundation for our nation. Charles should understand that, as a Christian country, we need to accept and acknowledge Christ alone as the Way, the Truth and the Life. As such, we value and respect the beliefs of others, but we do not accept them as of equal standing and value. We do not all worship the same God.

We applaud our new King's efforts to unify the nation, and we unreservedly support him in this, but we call upon him to reaffirm our nation's commitment to Christian values and belief. Under Christ alone, who calls us to love and respect all equally, will our nation prosper, and only in allegiance to Him will we demonstrate and achieve genuine tolerance. Let us not compromise our fundamental and foundational beliefs out of failure to appreciate and acknowledge the differences between different religions – or indeed between religion and secularism – and for fear of offending those who pursue a different, and inconsistent agenda.

In recent years, Christianity has become the most persecuted faith on the planet. From Afghanistan to North Korea, to India and Iran, to Somalia, Egypt, Pakistan, China … the list seems endless, but in all these countries Christians now face discrimination, injustice, intimidation, mistreatment, abuse, violence, ethnic cleansing and even genocide. In truth, Christians receive neither tolerance nor respect from other faiths. So let us not delude ourselves that we shall achieve a peaceful and harmonious society by sacrificing our Christian heritage and belief to what are essentially woke ideas of inclusivity.

We call upon our new King to uphold the faith courageously, valuing others, but without the misapprehension that they share a similar commitment to that love, tolerance and respect that is genuinely the heart of Christianity.

Source: Voice for Justice UK, 2022/ 23

b. Artificial Intelligence, New Religion & a New King

'AI could create religion in the future'. So warns Israeli scholar Yuval Noah Harari. Through manipulation of language and story-telling, he says, AI (artificial intelligence) could cocoon humanity in a Matrix-like world of illusions (https://www.thetimes.co.uk/article/ai-will-could-religions-to-to-control-humans-warns-sapiens-author-harari-fhbzgbv7b).

He is no doubt right, except for one vital point, which appears to have escaped this bestselling historian and philosopher – Christian faith is based not on story-telling and belief in myth, but on a living and vibrant relationship between the believer and God.

And this is something that AI, no matter how clever it becomes, will never be able to replicate.

Yes, illusion can be both powerful and confusing, and the possibility that AI might in the future be able to exercise some form of malign mind control over those susceptible to suggestion must be acknowledged. 'Religions', after all, come in many shapes and sizes, and some are already based on delusion. But Christianity is different in kind. In Christ, and Christ alone, we are redeemed from bondage to sin and death and restored to that relationship with God for which we were first created. We are saved.

The idea that super smart robotic computers will be able to 'create religion', however, refutes that, lumping all belief systems into one. It is an idea predicated on the notion that God Himself does not exist. That God is Himself, in fact, no more than one type of illusion among many. It is a version of Marx's contemptuous dismissal of religion as the opium of the masses, and it is wrong.

The Bible says, 'Whether you turn to the right or to the left, your ears will hear a voice behind you, saying, "This is the way; walk in it".' That was God's promise in **Isaiah 30:21**, and it remains His promise today to all who accept the Lordship of Christ. If we live in obedience, we shall be guided by the Spirit of God – and against that, actually, AI doesn't stand a chance. But the problems start when men and women reject God's lordship and try and go it alone, because then they place themselves outside His protection. And then they really are vulnerable to suggestion and delusion. To put it another way, when we reject worship of the One true God in favour of self, we fall – and, sadly, that is precisely what the majority of humanity appear to be doing today.

There are without doubt dangers, should we allow the unrestrained development of artificial intelligence. Without proper regulation, for instance, AI could all too easily take over a country's defence and weapons systems, and in such a scenario nuclear escalation could become frighteningly real. But the orchestrated enforcement of illusion in order to control less intelligent humanity, as warned by Yuval Noah Harari, would be a direct challenge to God, and that is something the Lord will not allow. Even though dealing with such presumption might possibly, in the process, destroy us too, God will assuredly move. We do well to remember the flood.

In May 2023, the United Kingdom celebrated the coronation of our new monarch, Charles III. From long before his accession, our new king has been vocal in his commitment to diversity, as a young man affirming his desire to be 'Defender of faiths', rather than just Defender of the Faith. He has insisted therefore that non-Christian faith leaders not just be present, but play an active role in his coronation, and in this he has been willingly supported by in the Archbishop of Canterbury, who has committed the Church of England to fostering an environment where 'people of all faiths and beliefs may live together freely' (https://blogs.lse.ac.uk/religionglobalsociety/2023/05/with-interfaith-elements-in-the-coronation-king-charles-iii-will-promise-to-defend-the-church-of-england-as-the-state-religion/).

Thus, for the first time in our history, Jewish, Muslim, Sikh, Buddhist, Hindu, Jain, Bahá'í, and Zoroastrian representatives have all played a part in proclaiming and crowning our King.

Yet despite this, the Archbishop still insists the service was Christian, and in the tradition of the Church of England.

It is true that we are a culturally diverse nation, and it is surely good to promote unity – but not at the expense of our heritage and beliefs. How can the supposed head of the Anglican Communion, charged with defending the faith, so casually jettison the core beliefs of Christianity? Beliefs that hold there is only One God, and we must worship no other - and that salvation is through Christ alone.

Such politically motivated compromise, by both King and Church, can only be a betrayal of Christ.

Charles clearly sees himself as ruler of the United Kingdom, valiantly spearheading change. But he ignores at peril the tenets of our belief. He is monarch by God's grace, and he is called to serve, ensuring the wellbeing and protection of the peoples entrusted to his care, certainly – but not by setting up what is in effect a new faith.

'AI could create a new religion in the future'? Forget that, Charles and the Archbishop of Canterbury are already there.

Source: Voice for Justice UK, 2022/ 23

6. THE LORD OF THE STORM

a. Lord of the storm

Economic chaos, turmoil in the housing market, energy crisis, Covid rates on the rise, hurricanes ... and the ever-growing threat of world war. Each day we see the emergence of new and ever-worse problems, and nothing we do seems to help.

But God can help.

Our Lord who walked on the water and stilled the storm could even yet calm the tumult, – if we would only accept His Lordship and repent the wickedness we have not just allowed, but actively celebrated. If we would only repent and ask Him to intervene.

> **"When I pray, coincidences happen. When I don't, they don't."**
> **William Temple, former Archbishop of Canterbury**

Source: Voice for Justice UK, 2022/ 23

b. Repent – for the Kingdom of Heaven draws near

Repent ... before it's too late. That's been the stark warning of Scripture since the time John the Baptist first strode into the desert, then baptised Jesus in preparation for his mission on earth. But now there is an immediacy we have never perhaps experienced before, because Christ's return is near. Time is short.

Selfishness and greed
Contempt for traditional family
Promiscuity
Abortion
Same sex marriage
Denial of biological sex, as made in the image of God
Consumerism
Lack of respect and compassion for others
Hypocrisy

The list goes on and on. By its evil, self-indulgent and self-focused choices, mankind has placed itself under judgement. When Jesus died on the Cross, He set us free from bondage to sin. To all those who accepted, and accept, Him as Lord, He has given the gift of life, restoring us, by the Spirit, to that direct relationship with God for which we were first created. But just because He died and rose from the dead does not mean that salvation is automatic for the whole of humanity. There is still a spiritual battle raging over the earth, with the devil fighting might and main to enslave as many as he can ahead of the Saviour's return, and to destroy creation. To enter into and have life, we need to choose.

But, sadly, so many in this generation have rejected God, opting instead for short term consumerist and self-serving indulgence, deludedly asserting it's their human right to have whatever they want, at the time of their choosing.

This is very far from freedom, and by no stretch of the imagination are such choices a 'human right'. Rather, it is the giving of allegiance to Satan, welding individuals into bondage to sin, from which by themselves they will never be able to break free. Such life-style choices can lead only to death, and it is because of this – and the growing power of evil that such choices have both enabled and fed – that God is now coming in power. In truth, what the Bible calls 'the day of the Lord' is very near. It is a day of glory and restoration – but it is a day that starts in darkness and suffering, as evil is rooted out, exposed, and dealt with.

For our own good, God will allow this present evil to spread only so far, because He loves us too much to allow us to remain in Satan's thrall. He has given us every last chance to repent and put our house in order – withdrawing His protection so that we might even now recognise and turn from the evil we have allowed.

Covid, escalating violence, the energy crisis, global financial collapse ... these are the sour and bitter fruits of Godlessness. But God holds the key. The good news is, He could stop the approaching devastation in a heartbeat – more than that, He stands ready to intervene and help – but He will only do so if we turn from our 'wickedness', back to obedience to Him, and ask.

Without doubt, there are dark times ahead for the whole world. Humanity is not going to hell in a handcard; rather it is hurtling towards it in the latest model hybrid SUV or Ferrari, and the brakes have gone. And it may well be true that the majority have gone too far down the road to turn back, so that judgment, in the form of world war, disease, famine, poverty, and the like, has become inevitable. But, for Christians, though we too face tribulation, there is nothing to fear, because, in and through Christ, we are children of God and have life. Whatever may come, we have the strength and protection of the Lord, and the promise of life to come.

For those caught in sin, there is still time, even at this late hour, to repent and to find life. But this world, with its corruption and evil, must pass, in order to allow the greater and better to come.

So, the message to all remains. Each one of us has a choice, and should choose to follow, not the crowd, but the Lord. Repent, therefore, while there is still time. Turn to the Lord, because in Him you will find love, healing, fulfilment, joy… all you need. Repent and choose life.

John 3:16-21 (NKJV)
[16] For God so loved the world that He gave His only begotten Son, that whoever believes in Him should not perish but have everlasting life. [17] For God did not send His Son into the world to condemn the world, but that the world through Him might be saved.
[18] "He who believes in Him is not condemned; but he who does not believe is condemned already, because he has not believed in the name of the only begotten Son of God. [19] And this is the condemnation, that the light has come into the world, and men loved darkness rather than light, because their deeds were evil. [20] For everyone practicing evil hates the light and does not come to the light, lest his deeds should be exposed. [21] But he who does the truth comes to the light, that his deeds may be clearly seen, that they have been done in God."

Source: Voice for Justice UK, 2022/ 23

CHAPTER 6

False Religions and Occults

We are living at a time where multi-culturalism and multi-religions have been allowed into once called Christian nations. This has been allowed to happen slowly since the 1950's by successive non-Christian governments and liberal movements.

Some would say that it's good to have a diverse mix of people's and cultures, especially surrounding employment, helping countries growth and its wider economy, however there are many red flags, particularly the promotion of false religions and occults.

We seem to see this within the United Kingdom, where tolerance is expected for non-Christian religions, within its borders, however the Christian faith seems to be declining or replaced by humanistic christians, who seem to be led by social, liberal, cultural, environmental, financial movements and government pressures; instead of following the Christian faith, given by God freely to all mankind.

The ten commandments were written by God not only for the Israelite nation, but for the entire human race (to the very end), giving us all a set of instructions on how we should live, by honouring and obeying God, being obedient to our Heavenly Father, always relying on Him!

The Ten Commandments are an illustration of God's love He has for His people.

Read: *Exodus 20:1-21 NKJV,* **The Ten Commandments**

This chapter will now concentrate on illustrating those false religions and occults, where mankind disobeyed God in the garden of Eden following the lie (the enemy Satan). Until we accept that Jesus Christ is the Son of the Living God and that through believing and accepting Him into our lives, eternal life is promised to all everyone.

This is illustrated in *Genesis chapter(s) 1:26-28 and Chapter 3, NKJV.*

There are over 67 biblical verses relating to the practising of false religions: These are shown:

	Old Testament Verse(s):-
1	**Leviticus 17:7:** They shall no more offer their sacrifices to demons, after whom they have played the harlot. This shall be a statute forever for them throughout their generations.
2	**Leviticus 18:21:** And you shall not let any of your descendants pass through *the fire* to Molech, nor shall you profane the name of your God: I *am* the Lord.
3	**Numbers 25:1-2** Now Israel remained in Acacia Grove, and the people began to commit harlotry with the women of Moab. ² They invited the people to the sacrifices of their gods, and the people ate and bowed down to their gods.
4	**Numbers 25:3** So Israel was joined to Baal of Peor, and the

	anger of the Lord was aroused against Israel.
5	**Deuteronomy 4:28:** And there you will serve gods, the work of men's hands, wood and stone, which neither see nor hear nor eat nor smell.
6	**Deuteronomy 12:30:** take heed to yourself that you are not ensnared to follow them, after they are destroyed from before you, and that you do not inquire after their gods, saying, 'How did these nations serve their gods? I also will do likewise.'
7	**Deuteronomy 32:17:** They sacrificed to demons, not to God, *To gods* they did not know, To new *gods*, new arrivals That your fathers did not fear.
8	**Judges 10:14:** Go and cry out to the gods which you have chosen; let them deliver you in your time of distress.
9	**1 Samuel 12:21:** And do not turn aside; for *then you would go* after empty things which cannot profit or deliver, for they *are* nothing.
10	**1 Kings 13:1-3:** And behold, a man of God went from Judah to Bethel by the word of the Lord, and Jeroboam stood by the altar to burn incense. ² Then he cried out against the altar by the word of the Lord, and said, "O altar, altar! Thus says the Lord: 'Behold, a child, Josiah by name, shall be born to the house of David; and on you he shall sacrifice the priests of the high places who burn incense on you, and men's bones shall be burned on you.' " ³ And he gave a sign the same day, saying, "This *is* the sign which the Lord has spoken: Surely the altar shall split apart, and the ashes on it shall be poured out."
11	**1 Kings 14:23-24:** For they also built for themselves high places, *sacred* pillars, and wooden images on every high hill

	and under every green tree. ²⁴ And there were also perverted persons in the land. They did according to all the abominations of the nations which the Lord had cast out before the children of Israel.
12	**1 Kings 18:29:** And when midday was past, they prophesied until the *time* of the offering of the *evening* sacrifice. But *there was* no voice; no one answered, no one paid attention.
13	**2 Kings 17:15:** And they rejected His statutes and His covenant that He had made with their fathers, and His testimonies which He had testified against them; they followed idols, became idolaters, and *went* after the nations who *were* all around them, *concerning* whom the Lord had charged them that they should not do like them.
14	**2 Kings 17:17:** And they caused their sons and daughters to pass through the fire, practiced witchcraft and soothsaying, and sold themselves to do evil in the sight of the Lord, to provoke Him to anger.
15	**2 Kings 17:18-23:** Therefore, the Lord was very angry with Israel, and removed them from His sight; there was none left but the tribe of Judah alone. ¹⁹ Also Judah did not keep the commandments of the Lord their God, but walked in the statutes of Israel which they made. ²⁰ And the Lord rejected all the descendants of Israel, afflicted them, and delivered them into the hand of plunderers, until He had cast them from His sight. ²¹ For He tore Israel from the house of David, and they made Jeroboam the son of Nebat king. Then Jeroboam drove Israel from following the Lord, and made them commit a great sin. ²² For the children of Israel walked in all the sins of Jeroboam which he did; they did not depart from them, ²³ until the Lord removed Israel out of His sight, as He had said by all

	His servants the prophets. So Israel was carried away from their own land to Assyria, *as it is* to this day.
16	**2 Kings 19:12**: Have the gods of the nations delivered those whom my fathers have destroyed, Gozan and Haran and Rezeph, and the people of Eden who *were* in Telassar?
17	**2 Kings 21:3**: For he rebuilt the high places which Hezekiah his father had destroyed; he raised up altars for Baal, and made a wooden image, as Ahab king of Israel had done; and he worshiped all the host of heaven and served them.
18	**2 Chronicles 33:5**: And he built altars for all the host of heaven in the two courts of the house of the Lord.
19	**Psalm 106:37-38**: [37] They even sacrificed their sons And their daughters to demons, [38] And shed innocent blood, The blood of their sons and daughters, Whom they sacrificed to the idols of Canaan; And the land was polluted with blood.
20	**Psalm 106:39**: Thus they were defiled by their own works, And played the harlot by their own deeds.
21	**Psalm 115:4-7**: [4] Their idols *are* silver and gold, The work of men's hands. [5] They have mouths, but they do not speak; Eyes they have, but they do not see; [6] They have ears, but they do not hear; Noses they have, but they do not smell; [7] They have hands, but they do not handle; Feet they have, but they do not walk; Nor do they mutter through their throat.
22	**Psalm 115:8**: Those who make them are like them; *So is* everyone who trusts in them.

23	**Psalm 135:15-17:** ¹⁵ The idols of the nations *are* silver and gold, The work of men's hands. ¹⁶ They have mouths, but they do not speak; Eyes they have, but they do not see; ¹⁷ They have ears, but they do not hear; Nor is there *any* breath in their mouths.
24	**Psalm 135:18:** Those who make them are like them; *So is* everyone who trusts in them.
25	**Isaiah 44:13-20:** ¹³ The craftsman stretches out *his* rule, He marks one out with chalk; He fashions it with a plane, He marks it out with the compass, And makes it like the figure of a man, According to the beauty of a man, that it may remain in the house. ¹⁴ He cuts down cedars for himself, And takes the cypress and the oak; He secures *it* for himself among the trees of the forest. He plants a pine, and the rain nourishes *it*. ¹⁵ Then it shall be for a man to burn, For he will take some of it and warm himself; Yes, he kindles *it* and bakes bread; Indeed he makes a god and worships *it*; He makes it a carved image, and falls down to it. ¹⁶ He burns half of it in the fire; With this half he eats meat; He roasts a roast, and is satisfied. He even warms *himself* and says, "Ah! I am warm, I have seen the fire." ¹⁷ And the rest of it he makes into a god,

	His carved image. He falls down before it and worships *it*, Prays to it and says, "Deliver me, for you *are* my god!" ¹⁸ They do not know nor understand; For He has shut their eyes, so that they cannot see, *And* their hearts, so that they cannot understand. ¹⁹ And no one considers in his heart, Nor *is there* knowledge nor understanding to say, "I have burned half of it in the fire, Yes, I have also baked bread on its coals; I have roasted meat and eaten *it*; And shall I make the rest of it an abomination? Shall I fall down before a block of wood?" ²⁰ He feeds on ashes; A deceived heart has turned him aside; And he cannot deliver his soul, Nor say, "*Is there* not a lie in my right hand?"
26	**Isaiah 16:12:** And it shall come to pass, When it is seen that Moab is weary on the high place, That he will come to his sanctuary to pray; But he will not prevail.
27	**Isaiah 37:12:** Have the gods of the nations delivered those whom my fathers have destroyed, Gozan and Haran and Rezeph, and the people of Eden who *were* in Telassar?
28	**Isaiah 44:10-16:** ¹⁰ Who would form a god or mold an image *That* profits him nothing? ¹¹ Surely all his companions would be ashamed; And the workmen, they *are* mere men. Let them all be gathered together, Let them stand up;

	Yet they shall fear, They shall be ashamed together. ¹² The blacksmith with the tongs works one in the coals, Fashions it with hammers, And works it with the strength of his arms. Even so, he is hungry, and his strength fails; He drinks no water and is faint. ¹³ The craftsman stretches out *his* rule, He marks one out with chalk; He fashions it with a plane, He marks it out with the compass, And makes it like the figure of a man, According to the beauty of a man, that it may remain in the house. ¹⁴ He cuts down cedars for himself, And takes the cypress and the oak; He secures *it* for himself among the trees of the forest. He plants a pine, and the rain nourishes *it*. ¹⁵ Then it shall be for a man to burn, For he will take some of it and warm himself; Yes, he kindles *it* and bakes bread; Indeed he makes a god and worships *it*; He makes it a carved image, and falls down to it. ¹⁶ He burns half of it in the fire; With this half he eats meat; He roasts a roast, and is satisfied. He even warms *himself* and says, "Ah! I am warm, I have seen the fire."
29	**Isaiah 44:17-20:** ¹⁷ And the rest of it he makes into a god, His carved image.

	He falls down before it and worships *it*,
	Prays to it and says,
	"Deliver me, for you *are* my god!"
	[18] They do not know nor understand;
	For He has shut their eyes, so that they cannot see,
	And their hearts, so that they cannot understand.
	[19] And no one considers in his heart,
	Nor *is there* knowledge nor understanding to say,
	"I have burned half of it in the fire,
	Yes, I have also baked bread on its coals;
	I have roasted meat and eaten *it*;
	And shall I make the rest of it an abomination?
	Shall I fall down before a block of wood?"
	[20] He feeds on ashes;
	A deceived heart has turned him aside;
	And he cannot deliver his soul,
	Nor say, "*Is there* not a lie in my right hand?"
30	**Isaiah 44:9:** Those who make an image, all of them *are* useless,
	And their precious things shall not profit;
	They *are* their own witnesses;
	They neither see nor know, that they may be ashamed.
31	**Isaiah 45:20:** Assemble yourselves and come;
	Draw near together,
	You *who have* escaped from the nations.
	They have no knowledge,
	Who carry the wood of their carved image,
	And pray to a god *that* cannot save.
32	**Isaiah 46:7:** They bear it on the shoulder, they carry it
	And set it in its place, and it stands;
	From its place it shall not move.
	Though *one* cries out to it, yet it cannot answer

	Nor save him out of his trouble.
33	**Isaiah 57:13:** When you cry out, Let your collection *of idols* deliver you. But the wind will carry them all away, A breath will take *them*. But he who puts his trust in Me shall possess the land, And shall inherit My holy mountain."
34	**Jeremiah 2:5:** Thus says the Lord: "What injustice have your fathers found in Me, That they have gone far from Me, Have followed idols, And have become idolaters?
35	**Jeremiah 8:2:** They shall spread them before the sun and the moon and all the host of heaven, which they have loved and which they have served and after which they have walked, which they have sought and which they have worshiped. They shall not be gathered nor buried; they shall be like refuse on the face of the earth.
36	**Jeremiah 10:3-5:** [3] For the customs of the peoples *are* futile; For *one* cuts a tree from the forest, The work of the hands of the workman, with the axe. [4] They decorate it with silver and gold; They fasten it with nails and hammers So that it will not topple. [5] They *are* upright, like a palm tree, And they cannot speak; They must be carried, Because they cannot go *by themselves*. Do not be afraid of them, For they cannot do evil,

	Nor can they do any good.
37	**Jeremiah 11:12:** Then the cities of Judah and the inhabitants of Jerusalem will go and cry out to the gods to whom they offer incense, but they will not save them at all in the time of their trouble.
38	**Jeremiah 16:18:** And first I will repay double for their iniquity and their sin, because they have defiled My land; they have filled My inheritance with the carcasses of their detestable and abominable idols.
39	**Jeremiah 16:20:** Will a man make gods for himself, Which *are* not gods?
40	**Jeremiah 19:13:** And the houses of Jerusalem and the houses of the kings of Judah shall be defiled like the place of Tophet, because of all the houses on whose roofs they have burned incense to all the host of heaven, and poured out drink offerings to other gods.
41	**Jeremiah 22:8-9:** ⁸And many nations will pass by this city; and everyone will say to his neighbour, 'Why has the Lord done so to this great city?' ⁹Then they will answer, 'Because they have forsaken the covenant of the Lord their God, and worshiped other gods and served them.'
42	**Ezekiel 8:16:** So, He brought me into the inner court of the Lord's house; and there, at the door of the temple of the Lord, between the porch and the altar, *were* about twenty-five men with their backs toward the temple of the Lord and their faces toward the east, and they were worshiping the sun toward the east.

43	**Ezekiel 16:16-17:** You took some of your garments and adorned multi-coloured high places for yourself, and played the harlot on them. *Such* things should not happen, nor be. [17] You have also taken your beautiful jewellery from My gold and My silver, which I had given you, and made for yourself male images and played the harlot with them.
44	**Ezekiel 20:18:** But I said to their children in the wilderness, 'Do not walk in the statutes of your fathers, nor observe their judgments, nor defile yourselves with their idols.
45	**Daniel 3:4-7:** [4] Then a herald cried aloud: "To you it is commanded, O peoples, nations, and languages, [5] *that* at the time you hear the sound of the horn, flute, harp, lyre, *and* psaltery, in symphony with all kinds of music, you shall fall down and worship the gold image that King Nebuchadnezzar has set up; [6] and whoever does not fall down and worship shall be cast immediately into the midst of a burning fiery furnace." [7] So at that time, when all the people heard the sound of the horn, flute, harp, *and* lyre, in symphony with all kinds of music, all the people, nations, and languages fell down *and* worshiped the gold image which King Nebuchadnezzar had set up.
46	**Hosea 4:13-14:** [13] They offer sacrifices on the mountaintops, And burn incense on the hills, Under oaks, poplars, and terebinths, Because their shade *is* good. Therefore your daughters commit harlotry, And your brides commit adultery. [14] "I will not punish your daughters when they commit harlotry, Nor your brides when they commit adultery;

	For *the men* themselves go apart with harlots, And offer sacrifices with a ritual harlot. Therefore people *who* do not understand will be trampled.
47	**Jonah 2:8:** "Those who regard worthless idols Forsake their own Mercy.
48	**Micah 5:13-15:** ¹³ Your carved images I will also cut off, And your *sacred* pillars from your midst; You shall no more worship the work of your hands; ¹⁴ I will pluck your wooden images from your midst; Thus I will destroy your cities. ¹⁵ And I will execute vengeance in anger and fury On the nations that have not heard."
49	**Nahum 1:14:** The Lord has given a command concerning you: "Your name shall be perpetuated no longer. Out of the house of your gods I will cut off the carved image and the moulded image. I will dig your grave, For you are vile."
50	**Zephaniah 1:4-5:** ⁴ "I will stretch out My hand against Judah, And against all the inhabitants of Jerusalem. I will cut off every trace of Baal from this place, The names of the idolatrous priests with the *pagan* priests— ⁵ Those who worship the host of heaven on the housetops; Those who worship and swear *oaths* by the Lord, But who *also* swear by Milcom.

	New Testament Verse(s):-
1	**Matthew 23:13:** But woe to you, scribes and Pharisees, hypocrites! For you shut up the kingdom of heaven against men; for you neither go in *yourselves,* nor do you

	allow those who are entering to go in.
2	**Luke 11:52:** "Woe to you lawyers! For you have taken away the key of knowledge. You did not enter in yourselves, and those who were entering in you hindered."
3	**Acts 12:21-23:** ²¹ So on a set day Herod, arrayed in royal apparel, sat on his throne and gave an oration to them. ²² And the people kept shouting, "The voice of a god and not of a man!" ²³ Then immediately an angel of the Lord struck him, because he did not give glory to God. And he was eaten by worms and died.
4	**Acts 17:29:** Therefore, since we are the offspring of God, we ought not to think that the Divine Nature is like gold or silver or stone, something shaped by art and man's devising.
5	**Acts 19:26:** Moreover, you see and hear that not only at Ephesus, but throughout almost all Asia, this Paul has persuaded and turned away many people, saying that they are not gods which are made with hands.
6	**Romans 1:23-31:** ²³ and changed the glory of the incorruptible God into an image made like corruptible man—and birds and four-footed animals and creeping things. ²⁴ Therefore God also gave them up to uncleanness, in the lusts of their hearts, to dishonour their bodies among themselves, ²⁵ who exchanged the truth of God for the lie, and worshiped and served the creature rather than the Creator, who is blessed forever. Amen. ²⁶ For this reason God gave them up to vile passions. For even their women exchanged the natural use for what is

	against nature. ²⁷ Likewise also the men, leaving the natural use of the woman, burned in their lust for one another, men with men committing what is shameful, and receiving in themselves the penalty of their error which was due. ²⁸ And even as they did not like to retain God in *their* knowledge, God gave them over to a debased mind, to do those things which are not fitting; ²⁹ being filled with all unrighteousness, sexual immorality, wickedness, covetousness, maliciousness; full of envy, murder, strife, deceit, evil-mindedness; *they are* whisperers, ³⁰ backbiters, haters of God, violent, proud, boasters, inventors of evil things, disobedient to parents, ³¹ undiscerning, untrustworthy, unloving, unforgiving, unmerciful;
7	**Romans 1:25:** who exchanged the truth of God for the lie, and worshiped and served the creature rather than the Creator, who is blessed forever. Amen.
8	**1 Corinthians 10:20:** Rather, that the things which the Gentiles sacrifice they sacrifice to demons and not to God, and I do not want you to have fellowship with demons.
9	**2 Corinthians 4:4:** whose minds the god of this age has blinded, who do not believe, lest the light of the gospel of the glory of Christ, who is the image of God, should shine on them.
10	**1 Timothy 1:4:** nor give heed to fables and endless genealogies, which cause disputes rather than godly edification which is in faith.
11	**1 Timothy 6:20:** O Timothy! Guard what was committed to your trust, avoiding the profane *and* idle babblings and contradictions of what is falsely called knowledge

12	**Galatians 4:3:** Even so we, when we were children, were in bondage under the elements of the world.
13	**Galatians 4:8:** But then, indeed, when you did not know God, you served those which by nature are not gods.
14	**Colossians 2:8:** Beware lest anyone cheat you through philosophy and empty deceit, according to the tradition of men, according to the basic principles of the world, and not according to Christ.
15	**Revelation 9:20-21:** 20 But the rest of mankind, who were not killed by these plagues, did not repent of the works of their hands, that they should not worship demons, and idols of gold, silver, brass, stone, and wood, which can neither see nor hear nor walk. 21 And they did not repent of their murders or their sorceries or their sexual immorality or their thefts.
16	**Revelation 13:4:** So they worshiped the dragon who gave authority to the beast; and they worshiped the beast, saying, "Who *is* like the beast? Who is able to make war with him?"
17	**Revelation 13:8:** All who dwell on the earth will worship him, whose names have not been written in the Book of Life of the Lamb slain from the foundation of the world.

Timeline of False Religions, Doctrines and Occults

The following list contains those prominent false religions and occults, many of which are in existence today. They include:

	False Religions, Doctrines and Occults
1	1,500 BC. Hinduism- no specific founder
2	560 BC. Buddhism- Gautama Buddha

3	550 BC. Taoism - Lao Tzu
4	599 BC. Jainism, Mahavira
5	50-100 AD. Gnosticism-
6	150-250 AD. -Modalism (Monarchianism)–Sabellius, Praxeus, Noetus, Paul of Samosata
7	590 AD.-Roman Catholicism- Developed after Constantine; Pope Gregory.
8	610 AD.- Islam- Mohammed
9	1400 AD.- Rosicrucians-Christian Rosenkreuz (1694 US) Rosicrucians- Master Kelpius, Johann Andrea
10	1515 AD.- Protestantism- (Reformers) Martin Luther, Ulrich Zwingli, John Calvin
11	1650 AD.- Tibetan Buddhism-Dalai Lama
12	1700 AD.- Freemasony- Albert Mackey, Albert Pike
13	1760 AD.-Swedenborgism- Emmanuel Swedenborg
14	1784 AD.- Shakers - Mother Ann Lee
15	1830 AD.- Mormonism – Joseph Smith
16	1830 AD.-Cambellites-Alexander & Thomas Cambell, Barton Stone
17	1838 AD.-Tenrikyo- Miki Maegawa Nakayama
18	1840-45 AD.-Millerites 2nd day Adventists –William Miller then became 7th Day Adventists
19	1844 AD.-Bahai- Baha'u'llah (Abul Baha)
20	1844 AD.-Christadelphians- John Thomas
21	1845-1870AD.- 7th Day Adventists-E.G. White
22	1848 AD.-Spiritualism - Kate and Margaret Fox
23	1870 AD.-Jehovah's Witnesses- Charles Taze Russell
24	1875 AD.-Theosophical Society- H.P. Blavatsky, Henry Olcott
25	1879 AD.-Christian Science-Mary Baker Eddy

26	1900 AD.-Rosicrucian Fellowship-Max Heindel
27	1902 AD.- Anthroposophical Society –Rudolf Steiner
28	1914 AD.- Iglesia ni Cristo- Felix Manalo
29	1914 AD.- Oneness Pentecostalism- Frank Ewart, G.T.Haywood, Glenn Cook
30	1917 AD.-True Jesus Church. Founders Paul Wei, Lingsheng Chang and Barnabas Chang
31	1927 AD.- Mind Science- Ernest Holmes
32	1930 AD. -Black Muslims (Nation of Islam) –Wallace D. Fard
33	1934 AD.-World Wide Church of God- Herbert W. Armstrong
34	1935 AD.-Self Realization Fellowship- Paramahansa Yogananda
35	1944 AD.- Silva Mind Control –Jose Silva
36	1945 AD. -The Way -Victor P.Wierwille
37	1948 AD.- Latter Rain –Franklin Hall, George Warnock.
38	1950 AD.-Lafayette Ronald Hubbard published his book Dianetics-SCIENTOLOGY
39	1950 AD.-Urantia Book- Dr. Bill Sadler
40	1954 AD.- Unification Church- Sun Myung Moon
41	1954 AD.-Atherius Society (UFO's)- Dr. George King
42	1955 AD.- Scientology- L. Ron Hubbard
43	1958 AD. -Henry Kinley begins (IDMR) the Institute of Divine Metaphysical Research
44	1958 AD.- Institute of Divine Metaphysical Research- Henry Kinley
45	1958-1970 AD.- Church Universal and Triumphant – Mark and E.C. Prophet
46	1959 AD.-Unitariarian Universalist
47	1960 AD.-Enkankar- Paul Twitchell

48	1960 AD.-Transcendental meditation- Maharishi Mahesh Yogi
49	1961 AD.- Unitarian Universalism was officially formed.
50	1964 AD.- Eckankar *The Ancient Science of Soul Travel* (Eck). Founded by Paul Twitchell
51	1965 AD.-Assembly of Yahweh-Jacob Meyer
52	1966 AD.- Church of Satan –Anton LaVey
53	1968 AD.- Children of God- David (Moses) Berg
54	1968 AD.- Hare Krishna (US)- Swami Prabhupada
55	1970 AD.- Divine light Mission- Guru Maharaj Ji
56	1970 AD.-Findhorn Community –Peter and Eileen Caddy –David Spangler
57	1973 AD.- CARP was established in the United States. [The Collegiate Association for the Research of Principles] to introduce the teachings of un Myung Moon.
58	1974 AD.-Assemblies of Yahweh-Sam Suratt
59	1980 -1982 AD.- Tara Center-Benjamen Crème
60	1980 AD.- House of Yahweh (Abilene) Jacob Hawkins

The list shown is not conclusive.

Therefore, I would like to ask the reader, who do you believe in? Do you believe in the one true Living God and His Son, our Lord, Redeemer and Saviour Jesus Christ.

If you do, then good, eternal life will be granted to you. If you do not believe then I ask you why not.

For any other believe is false, and is of the enemy (Satan).

Therefore, those who do not believe will not inherit eternal life; but eternal death will be given!

Therefore, chose Jesus Christ and Eternal Life with the Living God!

CHAPTER 7

References

The following references are from the (NKJV) New Kings James Version Bible, and publications.

Please note that biblical references to the Bible, will be quoted back to that Book, and relevant Chapter and Verse i.e. Genesis 1:1 (chapter 1, verse 1).

Where only a book and chapter has been referenced, then this will be shown as Genesis 1.

All source(s) of information and links are correct at time of publishing.

References and source of Information:

1. 2 Timothy 4:1-5

Chapter 1 – Introduction

2. Genesis Chapter 1
3. Genesis Chapter 2
4. Genesis Chapter 3
5. 1 John 3:8, NKJV
6. Ephesians 2:8-10

7. John 3:15-21

Chapter 2 - GOD

8. Numbers 23:19
9. Genesis Chapter 1
10. Job 38-42
11. Revelation 19:6
12. Deuteronomy 31:6
13. Psalm 139
14. Proverbs 15:3
15. Job 34:21
16. Isaiah 57:15
17. Jeremiah 23:24
18. Matthew 18:20
19. Matthew 28:19-20
20. Luke 17:21
21. John 1:3-5
22. Acts 17:27-28
23. Colossians 1:16-17
24. 1 Chronicles 28:9
25. Job 28:24
26. Psalms 147:4
27. Psalms 127:5
28. Psalms 147:5
29. Isaiah 40:28
30. Jeremiah 1:5
31. Jeremiah 23:24
32. Jeremiah 29:11
33. Matthew 9:4
34. Matthew 10:30

35. Matthew 11:27
36. Matthew 12:25
37. Acts 1:24
38. Romans 11:33-36
39. 1 Corinthians 2:11
40. Hebrews 4:13
41. 1 John 3:20
42. John 3:15-21
43. 1 John 4
44. Genesis 1:26
45. Matthew 3:16-17
46. Matthew 28:19
47. John 1
48. John 5
49. John 14:16-17
50. John 14:26
51. John 15:26
52. 2 Corinthians 13:14
53. Philippians 2:5-8
54. Colossians 1:15-17
55. Colossians 2:9
56. 1 Peter 1:2
57. 1 John 5:7-8

Chapter 3 – Christian Principles & Values

58. John 3:16-21
59. John 17:2
60. John 17
61. Matthew 6:9-13
62. Deuteronomy 5:6-21

63. John 14:6-11
64. Matthew 6:9-13
65. Matthew 5:43-48
66. James 1:4-6
67. Mark 11:25-26
68. Philippians 2:2-8
69. Colossians 3:12-17
70. Titus 3:4-6
71. Ephesians 4:32
72. Hebrews 13:4-6

Chapter 4 – Establishment of the Christian Church

73. Acts 11:1-18
74. Acts 11:19-26
75. Acts 13-14; 15:39-18:22
76. John 14:6-11
77. Ephesians 5:22-33
78. Isaiah 5:20
79. 2 Timothy 4:1-5
80. Matthew 24
81. Revelation 1
82. Revelation 2
83. Revelation 3

Chapter 5

84. Isaiah 5:20-23
85. Exodus 20:13
86. Exodus 35:2
87. Leviticus 11:10-12

88. Leviticus 11:13
89. Leviticus 11:20
90. Leviticus 11:23
91. Leviticus 11:41
92. Leviticus 11:42
93. Leviticus 18:22
94. Leviticus 18:29
95. Leviticus 20:13
96. Leviticus 20:14
97. Deuteronomy 7:25-26
98. Deuteronomy 12:31
99. Deuteronomy 18:12
100. Deuteronomy 22:5
101. Deuteronomy 22:23-24
102. Deuteronomy 24:1-4
103. Deuteronomy 25:13-16
104. Deuteronomy 25:16
105. Deuteronomy 27:15
106. Proverbs 3:32
107. Proverbs 6:16-19
108. Proverbs 8:13
109. Proverbs 11:1
110. Proverbs 11:20
111. Proverbs 12:22
112. Proverbs 13:19
113. Proverbs 15:8
114. Proverbs 16:5
115. Proverbs 17:15
116. Proverbs 20:10
117. Proverbs 24:9
118. Proverbs 28:9

119. Proverbs 29:27
120. Jeremiah 32:34
121. Ezekiel 8:6
122. Ezekiel 22:11
123. Daniel 12:11
124. Daniel 9:27
125. Matthew 24:15
126. Mark 7:20-23
127. Mark 13:14
128. Luke 16:15
129. Romans 1:18-32
130. 1 Corinthians 6:9
131. Galatians 3:23-25
132. Revelation 21:8
133. Revelation 21:27
134. 1 Timothy 4:1-4
135. 2 Timothy 3:1-7
136. Romans 2:1-16
137. Revelation 19
138. 2 Corinthians 6:17-18
139. Galatians 2:21
140. https://www.theguardian.com/world/2023/feb/07/church-of-england-to-consider-use-of-gender-neutral-terms-for-god
141. https://researchbriefings.files.parliament.uk/documents/SN06988/SN06988.pdf
142. https://www.churchofengland.org/sites/default/files/2023-04/H%26F%20report%20DIGITAL%20SINGLE%20PAGES.pdf
143. https://www.churchtimes.co.uk/articles/2022/28-october/news/uk/we-will-conduct-same-sex-marriages-say-more-than-1000-clergy

144. https://www.churchofengland.org/sites/default/files/2020-06/Ministry%20Statistics%202019%20report%20FINAL.pdf
145. https://www.archbishopofcanterbury.org/news/news-and-statements/stephen-knott-be-new-archbishops-secretary-appointments
146. https://virtueonline.org/lambeth-deputy-become-archbishops-appointment-secretary-married-homosexual
147. https://www.anglicancommunion.org/resources/document-library/lambeth-conference/1998/section-i-called-to-full-humanity/section-i10-human-sexuality
148. https://www.thetimes.co.uk/article/church-of-england-christianity-survey-gay-marriage-sex-female-archbishop-70ck07sj6
149. https://www.premierchristianity.com/uk-church/exclusive-dissenting-bishops-speak-out-on-same-sex-blessings/16497.article
150. https://www.churchofengland.org/media-and-news/press-releases/prayers-love-and-faith-bishops-agree-next-steps-bring-synod
151. 2 Cor 6: 17 -18
152. John 3:16
153. https://www.christiantoday.com/article/more.divided.than.the.conservative.party/141054.htm
154. https://www.churchofengland.org/media-and-news/press-releases/synod-backs-trial-special-services-asking-gods-blessing-same-sex
155. https://www.dailymail.co.uk/news/article-12239043/Bid-ban-social-gender-transitioning-schools-narrowly-killed-MPs.html#:~:text=A%20bid%20to%20ban%20the,his%20proposals%20for%20new%20laws

156. https://www.washingtonexaminer.com/news/bud-light-dylan-mulvaney-business-sales-down
157. https://www.express.co.uk/comment/expresscomment/1756225/nike-dylan-mulvaney-trans-bra-advert
158. https://www.dailymail.co.uk/news/article-12098975/Calls-boycott-Adidas-womens-swimwear-advert.html
159. https://www.bbc.co.uk/sport/cycling/65718748
160. https://heightline.com/lia-thomas-height-how-tall-is-the-swimmer-and-what-is-his-current-weight/
161. https://www.sportskeeda.com/mma/news-when-transgender-fighter-fallon-fox-broke-opponent-s-skull-mma-fight
162. https://www.thepinknews.com/2014/09/20/martial-arts-champ-refuses-to-take-on-transgender-fighter-fallon-fox/
163. https://www.telegraph.co.uk/news/2023/05/28/let-women-speak-transgender-activists-protest-hyde-park/
164. https://www.telegraph.co.uk/world-news/2023/08/01/zhanna-samsonova-tiktok-instagram-vegan-diet-dies/
165. https://www.independent.co.uk/news/uk/home-news/costa-coffee-trans-man-mural-b2385455.html
166. https://www.england.nhs.uk/commissioning/spec-services/npc-crg/gender-dysphoria-clinical-programme/implementing-advice-from-the-cass-review/
167. https://www.ncbi.nlm.nih.gov/pmc/articles/PMC5178031/
168. https://www.ncbi.nlm.nih.gov/pmc/articles/PMC6830528/
169. https://www.mind.org.uk/media-a/2958/statistics-facts-2017.pdf
170. https://www.bmj.com/content/381/bmj-2022-073584
171. https://news.sky.com/story/hundreds-of-young-trans-people-seeking-help-to-return-to-original-sex-11827740

172. https://www.britannica.com/topic/pogrom
173. https://www.dailymail.co.uk/news/article-10549173/Now-Whitehall-told-ditch-Stonewall-amid-row-charitys-divisive-diversity-scheme.html
174. https://policyexchange.org.uk/publication/asleep-at-the-wheel/
175. https://www.ons.gov.uk/peoplepopulationandcommunity/culturalidentity/genderidentity/bulletins/genderidentityenglandandwales/census2021
176. https://www.gov.uk/government/publications/political-impartiality-in-schools/political-impartiality-in-schools
177. https://www.dailymail.co.uk/news/article-11702239/Christian-mother-sues-four-year-old-sons-school-saying-LGBT-parade.html
178. https://www.legislation.gov.uk/ukpga/1998/42/schedule/1/part/I/chapter/8
179. https://www.thetimes.co.uk/article/skirting-the-issue-school-uniform-names-go-gender-neutral-pmkbqp7tw
180. https://www.cfr.org/backgrounder/what-hamas#:~:text=In%201988%2C%20Hamas%20published%20its,Islamic%20society%20in%20historic%20Palestine
181. https://www.theguardian.com/politics/2023/oct/30/uk-ministers-cobra-meeting-terrorism-threat-israel-hamas-conflict-suella-braverman
182. https://www.thetimes.co.uk/article/iran-agents-uk-pro-palestine-protests-9f8pst6vf
183. https://www.bbc.co.uk/news/uk-67383065
184. https://www.dailymail.co.uk/news/article-12663819/Schools-sex-education-material-Education-Parent-asks-Secretary-Gillian-Keegan-warns.html

185. https://www.equalityhumanrights.com/en/human-rights-act/article-2-first-protocol-right-education
186. https://questions-statements.parliament.uk/written-statements/detail/2023-06-05/hcws814).
187. https://www.dignityindying.org.uk/news/royal-college-of-surgeons-drops-opposition-to-assisted-dying-as-survey-finds-majority-of-members-support-law-change/#:~:text=%E2%80%9CWhile%20the%20views%20of%20the,wishes%20of%20those%20we%20treat.
188. https://apnews.com/article/covid-science-health-toronto-7c631558a457188d2bd2b5cfd360a867
189. https://www.theguardian.com/society/2023/apr/14/netherlands-to-broaden-euthanasia-rules-to-cover-children-of-all-ages
190. https://www.dailymail.co.uk/news/article-11135637/Canadian-veteran-offered-EUTHANASIA-called-Veteran-Affairs-Canada-hotline-help.html
191. Deuteronomy 28:43
192. https://www.thetimes.co.uk/article/ten-million-residents-of-england-and-wales-born-outside-the-uk-2021-census-shows-jzh7pmplm
193.
194. https://www.gov.uk/government/statistics/sexually-transmitted-infections-stis-annual-data-tables/sexually-transmitted-infections-and-screening-for-chlamydia-in-england-2022-report
195. https://www.parliament.uk/globalassets/documents/post/postpn217.pdf
196. https://www.thetimes.co.uk/article/sex-education-culture-wars-driving-shocking-increase-in-std-s-among-children-times-health-commission-b7ds9zsmx)

197. https://www.telegraph.co.uk/news/2023/11/27/doctors-have-to-tick-whether-patient-has-a-penis-or-vagina/
198. https://www.thetimes.co.uk/article/trans-gender-guidance-schools-uk-published-7cnc0f596
199. https://www.telegraph.co.uk/news/2023/11/27/britain-faces-un-blacklist-over-trans-rights-lobby-ehrc/#:~:text=The%20UK%27s%20Equalities%20and%20Human,Stonewall%2C%20the%20controversial%20LGBT%20charity
200. Genesis 1:22
201. Genesis 1:28
202. Psalm 127:3-5
203. Genesis 1:26
204. 1 Corinthians 4:2
205. Mark 12:31
206. https://www.worldmeters.info
207. https://www.theguardian.com/science/2023/jul/27/scientists-july-world-hottest-month-record-climate-temperatures
208. https://www.thetimes.co.uk/article/ulez-expansion-london-high-court-ruling-2023-sadiq-khan-8h65kk8qx
209. https://www.euronews.com/green/2023/02/21/what-is-a-15-minute-city-the-eco-concept-that-has-been-jumped-on-by-conspiracy-theorists
210. 2 Chronicles 7:14
211. https://www.bbc.co.uk/news/science-environment-59039485
212. https://ukcop26.org/wp-content/uploads/2021/07/COP26-Explained.pdf
213. https://www.standard.co.uk/news/uk/boris-johnson-prime-minister-glasgow-downing-street-australia-b962342.html
214. https://news.sky.com/story/china-details-carbon-emissions-plans-but-offers-no-new-pledges-ahead-of-cop26-12443988

215. https://www.bbc.co.uk/news/science-environment-59049770
216. https://www.nature.com/articles/d41586-021-00659-y
217. Galatians 6:7
218. https://www.dailymail.co.uk/news/article-11220769/King-Charles-tells-religious-leaders-Buckingham-Palace-protect-space-faith.html
219. https://www.royal.uk/coronation-oath-2-june-1953
220. https://www.cambridge.org/core/journals/ecclesiastical-law-journal/article/coronation-oath/F83079759125218B8D97BA1722954CBC
221. https://www.bbc.co.uk/news/uk-england-leicestershire-62946146
222. https://www.thetimes.co.uk/article/ai-will-could-religions-to-to-control-humans-warns-sapiens-author-harari-fhbzgbv7b
223. Isaiah 30:21
224. https://blogs.lse.ac.uk/religionglobalsociety/2023/05/with-interfaith-elements-in-the-coronation-king-charles-iii-will-promise-to-defend-the-church-of-england-as-the-state-religion/
225. William Temple, former Archbishop of Canterbury
226. John 3:16-21

Chapter 6 – False Religions and Occults

227. Exodus 20:1-21
228. Genesis 1:26-28
229. Genesis 3:1-24
230. Leviticus 17:7
231. Leviticus 18:21
232. Numbers 25:1-2

233. Numbers 25:3
234. Deuteronomy 4:28
235. Deuteronomy 12:30
236. Deuteronomy 32:17
237. Judges 10:14
238. 1 Samuel 12:21
239. 1 Kings 13:1-3
240. 1 Kings 14:23-24
241. 1 Kings 18:29
242. 2 Kings 17:15
243. 2 Kings 17:17
244. 2 Kings 17:18-23
245. 2 Kings 19:12
246. 2 Kings 21:3
247. 2 Chronicles 33:5
248. Psalm 106:37-38
249. Psalm 106:39
250. Psalm 115:4-7
251. Psalm 115:8
252. Psalm 135:15-17
253. Psalm 135:18
254. Isaiah 16:12
255. Isaiah 37:12
256. Isaiah 44:10-20
257. Isaiah 44:17-20
258. Isaiah 44:9
259. Isaiah 45:20
260. Isaiah 46:7
261. Isaiah 57:13
262. Jeremiah 2:5
263. Jeremiah 8:2
264. Jeremiah 10:3-5

265. Jeremiah 11:12
266. Jeremiah 16:18
267. Jeremiah 16:20
268. Jeremiah 19:13
269. Jeremiah 22:8-9
270. Ezekiel 8:16
271. Ezekiel 16:16-17
272. Ezekiel 20:18
273. Daniel 3:4-7
274. Hosea 4:13-14
275. Jonah 2:8
276. Micah 5:13-15
277. Nahum 1:14
278. Zephaniah 1:4-5
279. Matthew 23:13
280. Luke 11:52
281. Acts 12:21-23
282. Acts 17:29
283. Acts 19:26
284. Romans 1:23-31
285. Romans 1:25
286. 1 Corinthians 10:20
287. 2 Corinthians 4:4
288. 1 Timothy 1:4
289. 1 Timothy 6:20
290. Galatians 4:3
291. Galatians 4:8
292. Colossians 2:8
293. Revelation 9:20-21
294. Revelation 13:4
295. Revelation 13:8

www.ingramcontent.com/pod-product-compliance
Lightning Source LLC
Chambersburg PA
CBHW041141110526
44590CB00027B/4088